MORE PRAISE FOR
AND *COU*

MW01001846

"With Barbara's guidance, I found the courage not only to write with honesty and compassion, but to submit my work. In her class, I wrote an essay (with her guidance and encouragement) that was accepted into an anthology for Random House. That led to my selling a book, which included stories spawned directly from the exercises in this book. It was as if I was writing the book all along — only in separate pieces. Barbara is a unique and inspiring teacher, smart, generous, encouraging, and skilled."

— Monica Holloway, author of *Driving with Dead People*

"Barbara Abercrombie is a truly gifted teacher — this book is her gift to the writer within us all, whether accomplished professional or raw beginner."

— Jacqueline Winspear, author of the Maisie Dobbs mystery series

"*Courage & Craft* is the perfect guide for anyone who has ever been passionate about telling a story but feels too frustrated, nervous, unsure, unworthy, clueless, or terrified to proceed. Barbara Abercrombie grabs hold of your hand, gently pulls you along, and doesn't dream of letting you go until you're steady on your own two feet."

— Jennie Nash, author of
The Victoria's Secret Catalog Never Stops Coming

"Barbara Abercrombie has been a hugely significant influence in my life as a writer. She taught me to take the critic off my shoulder and write without fear. She gave me the courage to take a short story and turn it into a novel that has just been published."

— Linzi Glass, author of *The Year the Gypsies Came*

"Barbara is an inspiring teacher — she understands the heart, mind, and soul of a writer and with positive and constructive feedback, brings out the best in her students. Barbara taught me more than the craft of writing. She encouraged me to persevere. I am forever grateful for her guidance and support."

— Nancy Minchella, author of *Mama Will Be Home Soon*

"Barbara Abercrombie was my first fiction writing teacher, and the best. I learned so much in her Courage & Craft course that I took it three times. All of Barbara's exercises were designed to encourage her students to take risks, to try different styles, to consider undertaking larger writing projects. We, who were at first shy of reading our work aloud, began to look forward to it, and to getting feedback from this kindest of tough critics. I left her classes inspired to go home and do what writers must, face the blank screen and fill it."
— Lisa Pearl Rosenbaum, author of *A Day of Small Beginnings*

"One of Barbara Abercrombie's writing students called her a Zen master of nurturing talent, dispelling fear, and communicating the art of writing. *Courage & Craft* is a true gift for aspiring writers. They now can experience Ms. Abercrombie's special combination of encouragement, candor, discipline, and sheer luminosity as a teacher."
— Linda Venis, director, UCLA Extension Writers' Program

COURAGE & CRAFT

COURAGE & CRAFT

WRITING YOUR LIFE INTO STORY

BARBARA ABERCROMBIE

New World Library
Novato, California

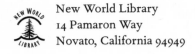

New World Library
14 Pamaron Way
Novato, California 94949

Sections on journal writing and the personal essay have appeared in different form in *The Writer* magazine and online at Barbara Abercrombie's website, www.WritingTime.net. "Dark Saddles of Greed" was originally published in the *Santa Monica Mirror*.

For permission acknowledgments, please see page 143.

Text design and typography by Tona Pearce Myers

Library of Congress Cataloging-in-Publication Data
Abercrombie, Barbara.
Courage and craft : writing your life into story / Barbara Abercrombie.
    p.   cm.
Includes bibliographical references.
ISBN 978-1-57731-601-5 (pbk. : alk. paper)
1. Autobiography—Authorship. I. Title.
CT25.A23 2007
808'.06692—dc22   2007024110

First printing, October 2007
ISBN-10: 1-57731-601-0
ISBN-13: 978-1-57731-601-5
Printed in the United States on 50% postconsumer-waste recycled paper

New World Library is a proud member of the Green Press Initiative.

10 9 8 7 6 5 4 3 2 1

For Brooke

Contents

INTRODUCTION

Here is my goal for you with this book: by the time you finish it you'll have written a crafted story about your life, either a short piece or the opening chapter of a book. Maybe your life is free and clear right now and you'll do it in six days, or maybe your writing will have to be wedged into an already full schedule of going to work or to school or both; taking care of kids, house, pets, family; and it'll take you six months. But the deal is that after years of dreaming about writing, or feeling stuck and unable to write, or not knowing what to do with your writing, you'll write something that has a beginning, a middle, and an ending. You'll finish a story or a chapter or an essay.

This book is about finding the courage to put your story down on the page no matter how disjointed it is or how sloppy your first draft may be, and no matter how revealing and personal it is. It's also about crafting your story, shaping and editing this piece of your life into an essay, memoir, fictional story, or family history. Writing is about discovering who you really are, where you've been, and where you're headed. It's about turning the messy, crazy, wonderful, and sad stuff in your life into something that has order and clarity and meaning — a piece of writing that other people can connect to and be moved by.

Only you can tell your story, your version of what really happened. Only you know what you heard, what the weather was like that day, the view out the window, the smells and sounds, the phone call, the hilarious moments and the dark ones, the adventure, the frustration, and what it was that made your heart pound. Only you can write about what changed, what will never be the same again. Only you can write what you felt.

Maybe the story you want to write is just one phase of your life, a memoir: your coming of age, becoming a parent, your divorce, the death of someone you loved deeply, or any passage of time or event that changed the direction of your life. Or perhaps your story is a short piece, a personal essay about frustration that turns into humor or a serious event that causes you to look under the surface of ordinary life. Or fiction might be the way to write your story, covering your tracks with a blend of the true and the made-up. Or maybe you want to tell it all in an autobiography — your whole life up until now, including a family history of past generations.

Whatever it is you want to write, it'll begin with you sitting down and opening a notebook or a new computer file. There will be no bolts of lightning, no muse floating overhead to tell you that the moment has arrived, that now is the time to write your story. Your parents, your spouse, your girlfriend, your boyfriend, your kids will not announce out of the blue that you have talent and beg you to begin writing immediately. You will always, *always* teeter between believing you have all these wonderful stories to write and worrying that the wonderful stories will not be very interesting. Nor will your life ever be in such pristine order that there will be endless worry-free hours in which to write.

You can sit around for the rest of your life dreaming about writing your stories, longing to bear witness on the page to every amazing thing you've seen or lived through, and wishing for a message from above, that bolt of lightning, some signal that will let you know now is the time to start being creative. Or you can just buy a notebook or turn on the computer and begin writing.

It's that simple and that complicated.

COURAGE & CRAFT

GETTING STARTED

MUSES AND JOURNALS

The scariest moment is always just before you start.
After that, things can only get better.

— STEPHEN KING

What I try to do is write. I may write for two weeks "the cat
sat on the mat, that is that, not a rat," you know. And it might
be just the most boring and awful stuff. But I try. When I'm
writing, I write. And then it's as if the muse is convinced that
I'm serious and says, "Okay. Okay. I'll come."

— MAYA ANGELOU

I asked the muse if she needed a ride. When she hopped in,
I couldn't believe my eyes. What a babe. I slid my arm
around her and cruised down the avenue.
Women waved; men nodded and smiled.
How proud I was to finally be a real writer.

— SY SAFRANSKY

Since it's highly unlikely that a kindly muse will announce from above that you should start writing immediately, and equally improbable that the people you love are encouraging you to write about the deepest, most personal aspects of your life, and since you might just possibly have this little voice in your head humming about your lack of talent or doing a riff on how real grown-ups don't sit in a room all alone still wearing their bedroom slippers and writing stories about themselves, and *Who would be interested in your story anyway?* — here's what you need to do: make up your own muse.

Make up a new voice that will inspire you, a voice that will say whatever you need to hear and will drown out all the other, negative voices, both real and imaginary. A voice that tells you that you have something unique to say. Something no one else has ever written before, and that if you don't write it, no one will — it'll be lost forever. Because this is true: you do have something unique to say, and no one on earth has written it the way you're going to write it.

The dictionary says a muse is a "goddess or power regarded as inspiring." We all need as much inspiration as we can possibly get, but until you've been writing for a while, or you take a writing course or join a workshop, it's not a good idea to have a real live person in your life attempt to fill the role of your muse. Real live people, especially those related to you by blood or long history, have the habit of saying the wrong thing and giving you a perfect excuse not to sit in a room all by yourself trying to write. In the beginning (to be truthful, *always*) you only want to hear one thing from your family or friends about your writing, and that is: *My God, this is brilliant, don't change a word.*

Your muse could be another writer, one you know or one you've never met — someone whose writing always inspires you and reminds you why you're so passionate about writing; a writer who makes you believe that writing as a craft is accessible, something that you too can do, and who gives you not only a kind of blueprint for your own writing but also the courage to start.

At the moment my muse and mentor is Mark Doty. On bad days, when I forget why I even want to write in the first place, or *how* to write, I open up one of his memoirs — *Heaven's Coast* or *Dog Years* — read a bit and think *yes*. This is what it's all about, being deep and serious yet inviting the reader in, being intimate and open but with emotion always crafted by language. Though I think of Doty as a muse and mentor and I love him, I've never met him. If he were to come to Los Angeles for a reading, I'm not sure that I'd go. I like our relationship just the way it is — his voice on the page and me reading his words and loving them.

However, I'm a promiscuous reader: I fall in love and change my muse often.

TO DO: (The best assignment you'll ever get.) Go to a library or a bookstore and browse. Dip into books. Find the latest books by your favorite authors. Find the kind of book, or collection of essays, that you want to write. Find your muse and mentor, your literary love. Check out or buy as many books as possible. Go home and read. When you're writing you can rationalize these book binges. You're acquiring essential tools for your job.

What if you can't find a literary love? You will if you read enough. Or what if you don't like to read? My friend, if you don't like to read, don't write. There's no reason to. You'll be able to stand the loneliness, the frustration, and the rejections of writing only if you are passionately, madly in love with books, with reading, with words. If your heart doesn't start thumping with anticipation when you walk into a library or a bookstore, if you don't rationalize all the reasons why you must absolutely order all those books online and damn the expense, if your idea of hell isn't being stuck on a plane without a book to read, then quite simply: don't write.

All of us who write belong to a community of like-minded people, and the glue that holds us together is our love of reading, of books.

As well as being good company for writers, cats and dogs can make good muses. (If you love animals, you'll understand. If you don't, just skip this.) My cats, Stuart and Charlotte, have listened to more bad prose read aloud, to more moaning about how hard it is to write, as well as to bizarre moments of my over-the-top optimism — and they never lose their cool. They never say to me, *Oh, stop whining, and find some real work,* or *Don't count your chickens, cookie,* or *Don't you think this might be a little too personal to write about?*

My husband is allergic to cats, so Stuart and Charlotte live in my office, and they greet me at the beginning of every writing day with enormous enthusiasm. Tails up, meowing to me to get going: *Showtime, let's write!* My two muses. They love me unconditionally. Even my writing. It makes them purr.

TO DO: Who or what is your muse? Write what he or she is telling you.

The complicated and sticky part of writing your life into story is that you have to connect to your inner life to do it, and it's so much easier to chug along on the surface of things. Just about any activity beats facing your own imperfect self on the page. You suddenly develop a compulsion to work out at the gym, clean the garage, put your CDs in alphabetical order, locate all your old classmates from junior high on the Internet, or — my personal favorite — cook enough hearty soup to get whole armies through arctic winters. Once, when I was really stuck in my writing, I dug up half the backyard to create the world's largest compost pile. Most any compulsive activity seems so much easier and more useful than writing.

It takes practice to write about personal things, and you need to find a way to write without any expectations attached. This is what journals are for — or notebooks, or diaries, or whatever you want to call yours. This is the one place you can forget about craft. There is no craft to keeping a journal, and that's the value of it. Anything goes. Whining, endless descriptions of weather, walking down memory lane, complaining about not being able to write, writing rants to people you'd never say to their faces, copying down quotes that you love, listing your favorite things, pouring out your dreams, frustrations, pains, joys, fears, and so forth — it's all fair game.

But intimacy on the page takes time, just as it does in any relationship. The novelist Gail Godwin wrote about feeling like a virgin when she started keeping a diary, but finally, after much writing in it, she felt as if they had an old marriage: "The space between us is gone," she wrote.

Most everyone has heard about the emotional and health benefits you get from keeping a journal; writing about feelings and traumatic events is good for you. But for a person who writes, there are two other vital reasons to keep a journal.

First, a journal can get you in the habit of writing regularly, of finding a time and a place to write. You're not just jotting things down at random on little pieces of paper (though this can also be a good idea): you have a notebook and you write in it every day. Five minutes, an hour. It doesn't matter. You're starting a habit. And while you may think you need great rushes of adrenaline and creative highs to write, the fact is that very little gets written unless writing becomes a habit.

The other reason to keep a journal is to have a place to record the details of your life — both your inner life and the surface details. Details can turn to gold when you're writing stories about your life, including the long, boring days when nothing seems to happen. It's all material, no matter what does or doesn't happen.

Florida Scott-Maxwell, who wrote short stories as a young woman and then a few decades later trained as an analytical psychologist under Carl Jung, began keeping a notebook at age eighty-two. It was meant to be private, but she finally allowed it to be published under the title *The Measure of My Days*. She didn't date her entries because she felt there were few external events in old age, but she used writing in her notebook to examine her life, to continue growing. In one entry she writes, "You need only claim the events of your life to make yourself yours. When you truly possess all you have been and done, which may take some time, you are fierce with reality."

If you type the words "keeping a personal journal" on

Google, 1,020,000 entries will come up. These entries cover every subject you could think of (and more) for a journal — relationships, diets, yoga, cooking, finance, travel, spiritual quests, sugar consumption, dreams, goal setting, beekeeping — including a list of the "top 10 miraculous benefits of keeping a personal journal." Given those million-plus entries and those miraculous benefits, you'd think there would be hordes of people keeping journals, a whole planet full of people writing in notebooks day and night.

But when I polled friends and students on whether they wrote regularly in a journal, I was surprised by the lack of enthusiasm in some of the responses. For more than half the people I questioned, keeping a journal was like going on a diet, something a lot of people talk about and start but don't stick with.

Sally emailed me: "My problems with journal writing are the following: lack of discipline; it's not fun but rather seems so boring — it's not as if I have anything exciting or interesting to say; how do you start — 'Dear Diary'? In other words, mental block; for what purpose do I keep a journal? I guess I should think about purpose."

In a workshop Louis wrote, "Funny, I am always giving journals to others who declare, "It's the perfect gift. Thank you so much!" But I don't keep one of my own. I'm not sure what I have to say is profound enough. Not sure I am deep enough and not sure I want to see what is there if I do go deep."

In class Suellen wrote, "I do not keep a journal. Several issues: lack of discipline; lack of privacy; lack of time, the right kind of undistracted quiet time. I WISH I had kept a journal all of my life."

Nancy wrote, "I wish I had kept a journal, but I didn't. My default is due to the fact that I kept a diary for a while in grade school, and my mother found it, read it, and ridiculed me. A more likely reason is my hunch that this stuff I'm thinking about writing is pedestrian drivel."

For most everyone who has ever thought about keeping a journal but hasn't, and for those who started but stopped, the bottom line is fear. Fear of writing boring, shallow stuff, of not doing it "right," of not having enough discipline, of wasting time because there's no practical purpose, of having your thoughts and feelings ridiculed by someone who reads it.

It takes courage to write down what you think and feel. But if you don't figure out a way to get past the fear and write the truth, what are you ever going to write about? Even if camouflaged by fiction, you'll be writing some truth of your own reality. And if you don't find a way to be disciplined about your writing and find the time to do it, how are you ever going to write anything?

Courage doesn't mean sudden, miraculous strength of character: it means doing something difficult despite the fear.

TO DO: Open a new file on your computer, or buy yourself a notebook. I personally like the spiral notebooks you can buy at the supermarket or in the drugstore. It's easy to tear out a page if you want to, and you can more or less hide them in plain sight. The journals with lovely covers and heavy paper make me nervous; they seem to require that something deep and important be written in them.

There's a Japanese word, *kaizen*, which means making a big change by making one small change every day, doing one little thing differently. If you start keeping a journal and write just one thing in it every day, just one short description of a room or a face or an animal or a flower, or an idea for a story, in three weeks you'll have twenty-one descriptions or ideas. (I read somewhere that it takes twenty-one days to form a habit.)

Equally important is that by writing one description or idea every day, you begin to look for the face or animal or feeling you want to describe or for the ideas. You're thinking, looking, and listening like a writer. You're paying attention, which is the most important thing you can do as a writer besides write.

In an interview May Sarton said, "For any writer who wants to keep a journal, remember to be alive to everything, not just to what you're feeling, but also to your pets, to flowers, to what you're reading. Remember to write about what you are seeing every day."

She begins one of her own published journals, *Journal of a Solitude*, with these words: "Begin here. It is raining. I look out on the maple where a few leaves have turned yellow, and listen to Punch, the parrot, talking to himself and to the rain ticking gently against the windows."

This is such a simple and accessible way to begin. Look out your own window and describe what you see. What kind of weather are you having today? What do you hear? I saw a collection of pictures once by a photographer who photographed the same tree every day for a year at the same time of day. Three hundred and sixty-five versions of the same tree! It caused me to really see a tree in all its subtle changes of light and growth.

TO DO: Try writing a description of what's outside your window for twenty-one days. Train your eye as if you were looking through a camera or had a paintbrush in your hand.

I began my own journal as an assignment in a writing class, and for a long time I just wrote descriptions of what I observed. A bird stalking through a puddle on campus. The weather. A stranger's face. It felt risky and messy at first to plunge into my feelings on paper. I was thirty-two years old, and after years of dreaming about becoming a writer, I was finally doing something about it. In my journal I wanted to sound like a real writer, not who I really was — a frustrated and scared writing student with two babies and very little formal education. It took months before I stopped feeling as if my critic were reading over my shoulder and I started writing from the inside out.

Even today, when I've been visiting or traveling with family and friends, I feel awkward getting back into my journal, into such a private space. It's as if I've been living on the outside and have lost a connection to my own inner voice. And that inner voice is the same one I need to connect with to write fiction or nonfiction.

I always think what I'm writing in my journal is boring. Even if something exciting happens, I think the way I write about it isn't doing the event justice. But I know from experience that I'll reread what I've written in a few months or years and be surprised by the fact that it isn't boring at all.

Sarton also writes of the fear she felt when she was first

alone in her house after being with friends: "I feel inadequate. I have made an open place, a place for meditation. What if I cannot find myself inside it? I think of these pages as a way of doing that."

If you keep writing no matter what, you'll not only find discipline and a way to record the details of your life; you'll also discover yourself in the pages of your journal.

TO DO: Guided imagery — close your eyes, take a few deep, measured breaths, and think about what keeps you from writing. Imagine it as an object. Give this thing that keeps you from writing a color, a shape, a texture, a temperature, a sound. Maybe it's all sound — the voice of a parent or a teacher. Pay attention to how this object or voice makes you feel. Then write about it. (My students have imagined everything from steep black walls to pillows over their faces, gray slippery rocks to lectures from parents and teachers. When we started doing this exercise in class, I was surprised to discover that many of the descriptions of objects had the energy and imagery of poems.)

Maybe you're working hard at juggling a full-time job, business travel, friends and family, a dog and a cat, and a million daily details, and you're thinking the last thing you need right now is one more item on your to-do list. You assure yourself that when things calm down, when your life is more organized, then you'll write. Someday.

Or maybe you're home taking care of small children, up to your elbows in diapers and peanut butter and jelly sandwiches, with a thousand Lego pieces underfoot, and you're thinking,

Who would ever want to read about this? You haven't had an adult conversation in days, and your vocabulary seems to consist of one-word commands and discussions with very short people about pooping and not biting, and you're thinking someday you'll write, when there's more to write about, more time, more energy.

For most of us, things will never calm down, we will never get organized, and there will never be enough time and energy. But there are ways to be creative by keeping track of your life during hectic times. A journal doesn't always have to be a note-book or a computer file. It could also be a box or an envelope to keep those jottings on little pieces of paper, or a collection of daily email messages or letters, or any trick you can find to slip into writing every day, if only for ten minutes.

You could send your best friend, or your parents, a daily email about what the kids are up to. Or when you're doing email late at night after work, send yourself a quick message about something you observed or thought about during the day.

When my first husband was in the U.S. Navy and stationed on a ship off the coast of Vietnam for six months, I wrote him a letter every day. I was living in a suburb of San Diego with our two baby daughters, so there wasn't anything wildly exciting to write about. I took care of the babies, went grocery shopping, cleaned my house, visited friends, tried to write, and read a lot. I thought my letters were full of the most ordinary, dull details ever put to paper. *This is what Gillan said to the Safeway check-out person, this is what Brooke said at breakfast about oatmeal, this is what we had for dinner, this is how it feels to drag the trash barrel out to the curb Tuesday nights and look up at the moon.* Years later when I reread those letters, I realized how precious that time was, and I hadn't lost it, thanks to all those ordinary details saved in writing.

One reason to write is to own, literally and figuratively, the moments of your life.

TO DO: Write down five minutes' worth of the ordinary details of today. It can be a list.

RUNNING IN THE DARK

I get up every morning very early and run. I don't run fast or far, and sometimes I just walk — but I'm out there. Each night I leave my running clothes in the bathroom all set out so that I don't have to decide what to wear or give myself the excuse that this is all too complicated and I should go back to bed because I can't find my socks or a sweatshirt. I like to run just before dawn, when it's still dark out and I can't see clearly how far I have to go before I can turn around and head back home.

I never leap out of bed dying to run, any more than I race to my desk dying to write every morning. Both are something I do because I feel awful when I don't. Being disciplined is never pleasant until you're into it or it's over. And I think the main element in discipline is not strength of character but sheer stubbornness. In both running and writing, once I get going it's okay, and sometimes it's even fun. But the point is the habit, the doing it when I want to stay in bed or do anything at all rather than write.

Another point for me is the dark. It focuses me when I can't see my turnaround point, where it's going to end. I can run twice the distance in the dark that I can in the light. No one is watching. I get in my own way when I can see how far I've come, how much farther I have to go. I start thinking too much, getting self-conscious, judging myself.

Running in the dark is like doing a quick write — a five-minute writing exercise sometimes called automatic writing or free writing. To do this exercise you take a topic, a sentence, or one word, and timing yourself for five minutes, you start writing. The only "rule" is that your pen, pencil, or fingers on the computer keys can't stop moving.

You don't think. You have no idea what you're going to write — you're running blind in the dark and you just write whatever comes into your head. If the subject or word you've given yourself to write about stops you dead in your tracks, you write your way out of it by writing about being stopped dead in your tracks. You can write anything during this exercise; just don't stop writing. If you stop to erase something, or pause to think, you'll get in your own way; you'll worry about your grammar or the right word or if it's boring or what somebody else is going to think of it. Even if you're writing nonsense or what you're going to have for lunch, you're writing. And writing leads to more writing.

TO DO: Write about the room you're in. Five minutes. What are your five senses picking up? Don't think; don't comment. Just write the details. What's outside the window? Is the radio on? Can you hear traffic? Birds? The hum of a computer? What color are the walls? What smells are in the room — cooking from another apartment, your coffee, city smells, country? Are you drinking water, a Coke? Smoking? Chewing gum, your nails? Which way does the light slant? How does your pen feel in your hand, or the computer keys under your fingertips? Maybe you're not in a room — you're outside on a bus, in a parked car, sitting in the grass or on a park bench. Write about the landscape around you, the people you see. You don't need conclusions or opinions, just the concrete details.

Think of driving a car. What if you got behind the wheel and you thought through each step: *Right hand now reaching for ignition, going from park into drive, checking rearview mirror, right foot on gas pedal.* I haven't driven like that since I took my first driving test at age sixteen and ended up on the curb, failing the test. Driving is like running or making love or writing first drafts. Thinking adds nothing and just gets in the way. The same is true with the five-minute exercise. You have to get out of your own way.

You have a deep well inside you filled with memories, thoughts, feelings, fantasies, observations. You have everything necessary for your writing. Now you just need to get out of your own way and avoid curbs.

I've tried different timing for quick writes in my classes and workshops, and what works best is five minutes — not ten, not fifteen. The pressure is so tight — five minutes! You're writing at top speed, in a short blast of creativity, no pausing, and it takes a lot of energy. You're jump-starting yourself. Sometimes it feels as if you're in a runaway truck, heading for a cliff. But who can write anything worth saving in just five minutes? So you're off the hook. Anything you *can* use is gravy.

Sometimes all hell can break loose with this exercise. Things can veer off into subjects that you had no intention of ever writing about. Secrets spilling out all over the page. Places you didn't want to go, right over the cliff. But this is good, and you can always tear it up if you need to.

Sometimes you find out what you're really trying to say. And isn't that one of the joys of writing? Discovering what you really think and feel? Very often in class people will be surprised and embarrassed by their own sudden tears as they read their five-minute exercise aloud. "I don't know where this comes from!" they always say, trying to disown their own emotion about what they've written. It's like their subconscious is delivering up messages, and they're taken off guard when they read them aloud. That's what five-minute exercises can do: surprise you with your own life.

TO DO: Write about what you're afraid of when you write. Five minutes.

When Kent Haruf wrote the first draft of his novel *Plainsong*, he pulled a wool stocking cap over his eyes in an effort to get rid of the feeling that an invisible critic was sitting on his shoulder watching every word he wrote. "It's the old notion of blinding yourself so you can see," he writes in his *New York Times* essay on writing. "I'm trying to avoid allowing the analytical part of my mind into the process too soon. Instead, I'm trying to stay in touch with the subliminal, subconscious impulses and to get the story down in some spontaneous way."

TO DO: Write about the habits you have, good and bad. Five minutes. Write about things you do in the dark. Five minutes.

AND THEN WHAT?

A writer friend called me once, suddenly worried about what would happen to her journals when she died. She was in her thirties at the time and healthy, so this wasn't an immediate problem. But she wrote in her journal only when she was really, really mad at her kids (teenagers), and she didn't want them to feel that they had been unloved if they read her journals after she was gone.

She got me worrying too. The happier I am, and the more I'm working on writing projects, the less I write in my journal. When I do write, it's just a lot of did-that-went-there, including weather data. But when I'm not writing, or I'm going through a bad time in my personal life, my journal turns into my therapist. There's much more energy in my journal writing then — things get really personal and detailed, and much more interesting. There's also a lot of whining.

So like my friend, I thought about the future of my journals. My first attempt at keeping a record of my life began at age thirteen with a pink leatherette diary that had a little silver key that didn't work. I only wrote about teenage boys in it — what they looked like, what they said, what they did — with each comment or observation followed by rows of exclamation points. It was a five-year diary — a tiny space for each day, but relentless in its march through days and months and years. (Beware of journals or diaries with dated spaces — the space will be either too large or too small, and you'll feel guilty when you skip a day.)

A whole cabinet in my office is now filled with spiral notebooks, all the journals I have written since my first writing class. I have this vision of being very old, sitting by the fire, curling up with my cats, and rewriting hundreds of these notebooks. "What a graceful, sane, productive life she led," my grandchildren and great-grandchildren will say when they read them. "What an organized, calm, and nonjudgmental person she was." They will say this because I'll leave out all my neurotic moments and bad behavior.

Then I wonder: Should I leave one rewritten version, neatly typed out, plus the stack of notebooks? Or maybe I should forget about rewriting, just burn the journals and depart this earth in dignified silence.

But then I think, *Oh, if only I had my great-grandmother's day-by-day account of her life* — her did-that-went-there, along with all the moments of high drama and bad behavior in her life — what a treasure that would be.

The fact is, one reason you write is to have ultimate control over your own reality, so someday I intend to rewrite every word, if not to whitewash my life, then to at least leave a well-written version of it.

Remember, you keep the journal, not the other way around. Consider what you'll do with yours. Burning or tearing it up is always an option, but don't be too hasty. When I reread my pink leatherette diary as an adult, I was so disgusted to realize that as a teenager I apparently had the brain of a tadpole and was simply obsessed with boys that I threw the diary out. I regret it now, but on the other hand, I wanted to leave that ditzy teenager in the past. So you might say it was a cathartic move. But before you burn or tear up your journal, think about what it would be like to read the journal of one of your great-grandparents.

In a journal excerpt published in *Our Private Lives: Journals, Notebooks, and Diaries*, Joyce Carol Oates writes, "Very much out of contact w/ this journal. . . . A sort of revulsion re. the ego: who cares? So much data!"

Of course you can keep a notebook of just facts and observations, but you can also, despite possible revulsion for your own ego, write out every slight or trauma you've ever gone through. Writing nasty speeches that you'd never say in person is healthy. It's good for you to express anger on the page in an uncivilized, inappropriate way. A journal should be raw and messy. But don't rely on little silver keys to keep it private. The more secure you feel about the privacy of what you're writing, the more free you'll be when you write, so find a safe place to hide your journal.

When you write about traumatic events or huge milestones in your life, you'll get the energy and the feelings down, but in the moment it's unlikely you'll have the perspective. It's all raw data — valuable for its energy and detail, but it needs time to cool so that it can be shaped into meaning. During the bad times, just take notes.

Alice Sebold, in an interview with Terry Gross on NPR about her memoir *Lucky*, her story of being raped as a college student, spoke of the journal she wrote shortly after the attack: "It's like somebody taking a few moments out of being in the middle of a storm just to jot down the temperature, the angle of the wind, things like that. So it was all very factual, flat, uninflected writing that just told the facts of what was happening. . . . It was a way of waking up my memory."

TO DO: If you're feeling stuck, here's a list of ideas to write about in your journal for the next twenty-one days. Jump-start yourself with a five-minute quick write for each one and see where it goes.

1. What three things in life sustain you emotionally and spiritually?
2. How do you feel today (emotionally, not physically)? (If you come up with a word that can describe food, it's not a feeling.) How does this emotion make your body feel?
3. What ten things in life give you joy? What ten things give you pain?
4. How can you find more of the joy and less of the pain?
5. List five things you want. List five things you need.
6. Using the third person, describe yourself doing something.
7. What's the best thing that's happened this week? The worst?
8. What's the weather data for today? Sky color? Wind? Temperature?
9. Write a letter to an author you think of as a mentor.
10. Find a quotation that moves you and copy it into your journal. Why does it move you?
11. What three goals do you have for the coming year?
12. What do you want to be doing next year at this time? In five years?
13. What's keeping you from accomplishing right now what you listed in number 12?

14. Write an imaginary conversation with someone about an issue that's troubling you.

15. If you could change one thing about yourself, what would it be?

16. Describe a recent dream. If you can't remember one, make one up.

17. Describe something beautiful you saw this week. Describe something ugly.

18. Write about the best meal you had recently, and the worst meal.

19. Describe what you're wearing right now.

20. Start with the words: *My mother is/was a woman who...* And then: *My father is/was a man who...*

21. Write a letter to someone you love. Include a request, a regret, and an appreciation.

2.

PERSONAL ESSAYS

SHORT TAKES

Some years back, when one of my brother Andrew's funniest
essays was anthologized in a college text on humor, it was
accompanied by a series of earnest questions, aimed at
explaining to students just what the author must have had in
mind: "Since satire is meant to edify as well as amuse, what
lessons does Andrew Ward mean to teach us?" "What are
the stylistic clues that let us know he's trying to make us
laugh?" "Just what is the point of his essay?" That sort of
thing. Andy took the test — and failed.

— GEOFFREY C. WARD

We go into the self to escape the prison of self.
We are aware of the perils — both to ourselves and to our
hapless readers — but we wish to love the world; and the
world is terrible for those who do not know themselves.

— BARBARA GRIZZUTI HARRISON

BAD NERVES IN SUBURBIA

I used to have my high school essays returned with so many red notes in the margins it looked like the pages were bleeding. *What premise are you trying to prove?* Miss Clark would write in red. *Not logical!*

I just didn't get the formal essay. For me, premise and proof were as murky as algebra and chemistry, two subjects that had no relation, no connection to life as I knew it. I loved drama and emotion and the details of people's lives, and I didn't want to analyze or prove anything.

The first personal essay I remember reading was written by Joan Didion, published in *Life* magazine in 1969. It was the last sentence in the second paragraph that has stuck with me ever since: "We are here on this island in the middle of the Pacific in lieu of filing for divorce." The honesty and grace of this sentence stunned me. Here was a woman writing the truth, under her real name, writing about her husband and her little girl. She admits to "bad nerves" and sleepwalking through life. I remember reading the essay as I sat at my kitchen table in suburbia with my own little girls, my own rocky marriage, and my own bad nerves, in awe that someone could write her truth and then craft it into art.

I'm still impressed with the control in Didion's essay (later published in a collection of her essays, *The White Album*) — the way she shaped the personal and at the same time drew in the world: the possibility of a natural disaster, literary references, and the tension of her language.

You read personal essays to understand your life, to find

humor, to discover a new way of looking at the world. You write them for the same reasons. This kind of essay is about your journey through an experience, commonplace or traumatic — any situation you've felt strong emotion about — and what you learned or didn't learn from the experience.

You move to a new town, you go horseback riding for the first time, your dog dies, you try to order something online, you get a divorce, your youngest child goes to college, you have a car accident, you throw away your cell phone — anything you do, or think about, is material for a short essay. Rather than proving a premise, as in the formal essay my English teachers loved so much, you're writing about how you reached some kind of understanding and insight. Or maybe you simply came to awareness, or a humorous slant on something that previously had driven you crazy.

The trivia of life, the moments of crazed frustration, the small flashes of amazement and understanding are as much the subjects for personal essays as the milestones. Humor comes out of frustration, the things that don't go right in life.

Going nuts over weather and weight were the subjects of two published essays written by students.

Deb begins her essay about June gloom — weeks of constant fog and no sun along the coast in Southern California — with dialogue:

My friend went to Las Vegas for the weekend. He was telling me about seeing the latest hotel extravaganza there. But I was only interested in one thing:

"Did you see the sun?"

"Oh, yeah. It was so hot — 100 degrees, and I was sweating." He became giddy, remembering it.

"Does it still look the same?" I asked.

"Yeah, bright. And yellow."

Her voice in the essay is cranky and funny as she writes of other specific incidents during June gloom:

> Water cooler conversations are stranger, too: The marine layer is the cause of monkey pox; the marine layer makes us all look like cadavers; Hot Pockets are an excellent source of nutrition . . .
>
> The weather guy tries to explain it: The marine layer is basically a convection fog that occurs when warm land air moves out over cool ocean water. The result is moist, cool marine layers. It sounded credible, until the day he called it "Coastal Eddy." Which, of course, sounds like a bad lounge singer's name: "Catch Coastal Eddy . . ."

Phyllis begins her essay titled "The Trials of Living Life by the Numbers" with the numbers:

> May 26, 1949: 6 pounds, 2 ounces.
>
> January 1960: 93 pounds.
>
> June 1970: 140 pounds.
>
> August 1987: 165 pounds.
>
> September 1999: classified.
>
> As far as I'm concerned, I've just told you everything you ever need to know about me, because who I am and what I do is governed by numbers. In this case, it's the number registered on my Detecto scale. Appropriately, the name "Detecto" conjures up my deepest, darkest secret — my weight.

Cloudless blue skies and the perfect weight would not have turned into essays.

TO DO: Carry a small notebook or some index cards in your pocket or purse to write down your ideas for an essay. (As with those spiral notebooks for journals, I believe in the simplest and least-expensive small notebooks for taking notes. On the other hand, I have a writer friend who drools over all the expensive notebooks in the Levenger catalog. She swears she wouldn't spend forty-eight dollars on a little turquoise leather cardholder and get personalized note cards to put in it, but she does believe she might take better notes if she did. Whatever works for you, whatever you can afford, buy it and carry it around with you.)

I love to teach courses on writing the short personal essay because it's such an accessible genre. It's short, and everyone has material. If you're alive and breathing and can write a sentence, you can write a short essay.

You need a beginning, a middle, and an ending — a narrative. You're telling a story. The beginning needs to pull your reader in, to let your reader know in the first few sentences what the essay is about, as Deb and Phyllis do in their essays. Then something needs to happen. An anecdote illustrates your theme, what the essay is about. The reader wants to go through the experience with you, not to be told about it from a distance. Stick to the truth — you don't need to make anything up. Just by choosing the details carefully, figuring out what to leave in and what to leave out, you're shaping the essay.

The ending, the understanding and insight you gain, can be life changing or simply a slight shift in awareness. This is not a piece of writing just for reflecting or remembering; there's a point to it. Through your flash of insight or humorous take on something ordinary, the reader can connect and identify with either the experience you wrote about or the feelings you had. The essay has a theme, it's about something, and it comes to a conclusion like a satisfying story.

The first part of writing an essay is to find your subject and then brainstorm it on paper. Fling down everything that pops into your mind about the experience. This beginning step could be a list and then a very sloppy first draft, or a series of five-minute exercises, or any trick you can pull out of your hat to free yourself up for ideas. You don't need a glimmer of insight about what you got from the experience or the slightest slant on humor at this point. You're just writing your way into the essay. The most important thing is that you feel emotion about the experience — anger, frustration, grief, embarrassment, fear, love. If the emotion is pure happiness and contentment, you've got to dig down deep and write honestly about the cost, how you got there, because frankly, we don't want to read about perfection. Blue skies and perfect weight — there's no story there.

The word *essay* comes from the French word *essai*, which means "a trial or attempt." We read essays to find a new window to the world, to laugh, to learn something from other people's trials and attempts in life.

TO DO: Brainstorm a list of all the issues in your life right now, both huge and trivial. Maybe you're going through a milestone — a new baby or grandchild, a divorce, a marriage, buying a house, falling in love — and your list will reflect all the different experiences you're having with that event. Or maybe your list will be full of frustrations: catching up on email, dieting, encountering cat hair everywhere, dealing with a teenager, trying to keep a desk in order, owning a crazy dog. Lists are a great tool for writers because you don't have to feel inspired or creative to write one. A list doesn't carry the weight of commitment; it lets you off the hook. And unless you're in a coma, you can come up with a list of at least ten things.

When you have your list, choose one subject and write for five minutes. If you dry up on that subject, choose another one. If you get on a roll, just keep going.

Here's a list Rob wrote in class:

Tree trimmers (you get what you pay for)
Haircuts (you get what you pay for)
My 93-year-old painter friend who acts younger than me
    sometimes
Alcoholic friends
I say hi to anyone
No job: no self-worth?
The difference between change and loss
After an injury, girlie weights at the gym
OPB: other people's babies (scary but fun)
How to be the perfect houseguest

Rob's list had a lot of potential for personal essays. (In the end he chose to write about being the perfect houseguest and got it published in *Westways*.) Some ideas on his list could possibly be connected, such as tree trimmers and haircuts. And the difference between change and loss, and girlie weights at the gym.

TO DO: On your own list, see what ideas connect. You may be surprised.

In class John balked at writing the list of possible topics for an essay. He hated doing five-minute exercises. He told me he couldn't and wouldn't do them, but he finally wrote a list of ideas. Then he went home and at his own pace wrote a beautiful essay he eventually got published in the *Christian Science Monitor*. In the essay he connected his struggle with writing to his four-month-old daughter's ease with learning to communicate:

> So when I am at a loss for words, my skills inadequate for the job at hand, I try to remember the example she sets. My daughter knows there is a higher form of expression than what she is capable of now, just as I do when I'm stuck.
>
> However, while this knowledge can send me into a tailspin of doubt and self-criticism, she is largely unaffected by it. She just keeps on making her squeaks and squeals until they sound more and more like the sounds her mother and father make.

At the end of the essay he writes of a specific incident with his baby as she lay on her changing table and he tried to get her to repeat a few simple words:

> Her mouth moved a little in response, a sigh, really, more than anything else. But I had her attention. "I love you," I said, and smiled. She smiled briefly too, demurely, then got serious again.
>
> "I love you," I said. She paused, then opened her mouth. "Ah-loo," she said.

—⚮—

Sometimes essays come out of questions. When my first grand-child was born, I was stunned by how much I immediately loved her, and found that I was continually asking myself, *Where did so much love come from?* Until Emma was born, I had always been bored senseless by people who popped out pictures of their grandchildren with a long commentary on how brilliant and adorable they were. I'd think, *Oh, please, get a life*, and be overwhelmed by how terribly icky it all was.

By connecting my current question to this prejudice of mine, I had an idea for an essay. Opening with other people's photos of grandkids and my impatience with the general icki-ness of grandparents, then dealing with my question of the sudden love for Emma, and closing with telling her she was the most brilliant and adorable baby on the planet and sending photographs of her through the Internet to all my friends and thinking it wasn't icky at all, I had an essay.

Pay attention to your own questions about your feelings and behavior. Pay attention to your prejudices and the web of your own hypocrisy.

TO DO: Write a very sloppy first draft of an essay. This draft can be too short and too lean, or too long and overwrought. *No one will ever see it*. That seems so obvious — of course no one will see this sloppy draft you're writing unless you show it to them. But you can forget this obvious fact when you're writing and the critic in your head gets too loud. Tell your critic to set-tle down (his or her turn is coming up next) and just write your essay from start to finish. If you get hung up on something, write *XXX*s and keep going. Get it all down on paper no matter what.

The second step in writing a personal essay is to gather up your lists, your notes, and your sloppy first draft and start editing. This is where craft and structure begin.

Keep the essay short — aim for four hundred to eight hundred words, because this forces you to stick to the subject and makes the writing tight. It's also a marketable length, and the market for short personal essays is vast and varied. If you want to get published, this is your first step. (Essays appearing in literary magazines such as the *New Yorker*, *Harper's* magazine, the *Atlantic Monthly*, the *American Scholar*, or any of the smaller literary magazines are usually much longer — from three thousand to six thousand words — and much harder to get published.)

Use the devices of fiction: Set the scene. What were your five senses picking up? What was said? Use dialogue if you can. Be specific in your details and descriptions of people, places, and things.

Eight questions to ask yourself as you edit:

1. Does your opening get right to the subject of the essay? Will it draw the reader in?

2. Does the first paragraph set up accurate expectations for the rest of the essay? If not, cut. It might be lovely writing, but it's beside the point. (Often you need to write your way into an essay, and by overwriting you figure out what the essay is really about.) Try to recognize now where your essay truly begins.

3. Cut to the chase. Is your writing specific and concrete? Not "a beautiful day" but a specific day with

the sky a specific color, the air a specific temperature, or with certain smells in the wind. Find the one
detail that will nail that specific day, face, room,
meal. Cut all adjectives and adverbs that don't give
essential information. Focus on the verbs because
verbs are what carry the energy in your writing.

4. Does something happen in your essay? Is there
   forward motion to it, action, not musing? Is there
   at least one specific incident or anecdote?

5. Is there specific feeling or emotion in the essay? Do
   you care deeply about what you're writing?

6. Is the essay about something specific? Is there a
   theme? Does it have a conclusion? A point?

7. Is there a new awareness or change at the end (even
   if it's only the awareness of things not changing)?
   Or do you have a humorous take on something
   frustrating?

8. How does your essay sound when you read it
   aloud? Often your ear will pick up something that
   your eye misses.

Notice that four of those questions include the word *specific*.
In your journal your writing can be general, sprinkled with hundreds of overblown adjectives, but you need to be specific and
rigorous with your language in a crafted form of writing. This
isn't easy for any writer. It's why we rewrite and revise. It's why
the whole world isn't sitting at home in sweat suits in front of
computers churning out books. It's hard work. But it's okay that
it's hard work.

As I try to start writing a new project, I always feel like one
of those birds in the film *Winged Migration* headed north over

huge frozen fields, nothing but the sound of my wings flapping. Or like one of the penguins in *March of the Penguins*, with my little webbed feet crunching over frozen tundra. It's cold, there's a long, long way to go, and God knows if I'll make it.

The difference between having written for three decades and doing it for the first time is that I know writing feels like this, while you may think that if it's such a struggle, such hard work, then maybe writing isn't what you should do. Trust me, you have to do the hard work before you get to the exhilaration — your own north pole or wherever you're headed. And it's worth it.

TO DO: Cut to the chase in the beginning of your sloppy draft. Edit out all unnecessary words. Add specifics wherever you can. Ask yourself what the essay is about. (You might even write what it's about — one or two sentences at most — at the top of every page because it's easy to get lost in your own essay.) See if you can get it down to eight hundred words. Each time you rewrite, try setting the essay aside for a couple of days or weeks before you go back to work on it.

It's difficult to have perspective on your own work, even after a few days or weeks. I'm usually a very definite person; my opinions don't change without good reason. Except when it comes to my writing. At 8:00 in the morning a chapter can be glowing with promise. I read it and think, *Yes! Finally, finally I've nailed it.* I email my agent to crow about how well the writing is going. By noon I want to bury the chapter in the backyard. The whole thing has collapsed on me like a bad soufflé.

If you're lucky, you'll eventually find a person you trust, someone who has clear perspective on your writing and no personal baggage about you. This person has faith in you and your work and will simply be honest yet encouraging at the same time. If you keep on writing, maybe you'll find a number of people to be your readers, most likely other writers you'll meet in a workshop or class. I have a list of five (writers or passionate book lovers) who read my work before I send it to my agent. Sometimes I add more, depending on the subject I'm writing about. These people, all of whom are worth their weight in gold and rubies, have a calmer view of my writing than I do. They're generous but also honest and won't hesitate to let me know where I've gone off track. And I trust them.

—⁓—

One night at a gallery opening in Livingston, Montana, I fell in love with a painting. It just blasted off the wall straight into my heart, alive with color and energy, while all the other art on the wall next to it hung flat and lifeless. To my disappointment the painting had already sold. I knew the artist, Todd Conner, and when I saw him that night and told him how much I loved his painting and that I thought it was his best work, he said, very seriously, "But why do you like it so much?" I went on about the way he rendered light, the vibrant color, the energy, the subtlety, and he just shook his head. He was truly puzzled and amazed at my reaction. He's a modest man, but this was beyond his natural modesty about his work; he seemed to be asking for a key into his own art. What makes it work? Why is my best work my best?

Sometimes the painter or the writer is the last to know. Besides, your job is just to do the work.

"Don't always be appraising yourself wondering if you are better or worse than other writers," writes Brenda Ueland in her classic book, *If You Want to Write*. And she quotes Blake: "I will not Reason & Compare, my business is to Create."

PASSIONS AND OBSERVATIONS

The best way to learn how to write an essay, of course, is to read as many essays as you possibly can — both long, literary essays and the shorter ones that appear in newspapers and magazines. Read essays you love, and ones you don't. You can learn from both and can be just as inspired by the bad ones (knowing you could write one much better) as by the really good ones.

Here are some cut-to-the-chase openings of my favorite literary essays:

> "Over there, the red Jeep. Park!" Ben, my gentle Filipino driving instructor, has suddenly become severe, abrupt, commanding.
> — Katha Pollitt, "Learning to Drive," *New Yorker*

When Ben, the driving instructor, later points out that observation is her weakness, Pollitt takes this as a metaphor for her whole life, particularly her relationship with a man she's lived with for years who's just left her for a "drab colleague." It's an intensely personal essay about serious truths in Pollitt's life, but it's also hilariously funny, thanks to her self-deprecating wit. And she got a lot of literary mileage out of the guy who left her: two years later she published another essay in the *New Yorker*, "The Webstalker," which opens, "After my lover left me, I went a little crazy for a while."

> The widow wanted the cherry coffin. All she could think of was her husband, dead. Dead at 40 in the dead of winter.
> — Thomas Lynch, "The Going Rate,"
> *New York Times Magazine*

Lynch, who is both a poet and a funeral director, pulls you into his essay with a specific encounter with a young widow who wanted an expensive coffin. He uses this as a springboard for his theme: what really counts in life. (This essay is shorter than the other literary essays I've quoted from — about eight hundred words.) At the end he writes:

> Keep the difficult vigils — with the dying and the dead and the bereaved. . . . If you bury your people, bring the shovel, go to the hole in the ground, bear witness. If you burn your dead, warm to the fire, stay until it's over, bear witness.
>
> Spend what you have to — nothing more, nothing less. In the end, we all run out — time, money, words. . . .
>
> What counts? What lasts.

This is an ending you can reread and savor like a good poem.

—⁂—

A few months ago, my husband and I decided to mix our books together. We had known each other for ten years, lived together for six, been married for five.

    — Anne Fadiman, "Marrying Libraries," *Ex Libris*

Though the math in the second sentence is puzzling, the rest of Fadiman's opening is straightforward and is matched by an ending with the same satisfying clarity: "My books and his books had become our books. We were really married." Between the opening and ending she chronicles the sweet dilemma of combining the libraries of two passionate book lovers: "We physically handled — fondled, really — every book we owned." She includes all the problems of this merger — duplicate copies, dedications from old friends and lovers, organization (chronological or by subject?), marginalia, and so forth.

—⁂—

I shop every day. Most people don't. The service manager at the supermarket is worried about me. Whenever she looks up, there I am. "We're going to have to get you a job here," she says. "You're here enough."

    — Tim Morris, "My Supermarket," *American Scholar*

Morris, unable to bear to eat anything out of the freezer because of childhood memories of too-long-frozen, gray cube steak, writes about grocery shopping every day as if he's visiting the moon. It's one of the funniest essays I've ever read; everything in a supermarket is the target for his keen, quirky observation: "We have an aisle for Packaged Pasta, which implies that somewhere else in the store pasta is rolling around loose for the taking. . . . My favorite aisle, right next to Cereal, is Bars and Tarts. That's a hard-boiled aisle."

Notice that from the very first sentence you know what these essays are about, that expectations have been set up; there's nothing coy or clever or long-winded and explanatory in the openings. Things happen, scenes are set, and dialogue helps move the action along; details are specific and numerous; and the feelings are passionate. The authors care deeply for what they're writing about, whether it's the crazed desperation to learn how to drive a car, the disgust at the sight of frozen food, the love of one's books, or the spiritual side of being a funeral director.

TO DO: Write about shopping for food. Write about learning how to do something new that becomes a metaphor for another part of your life.

I have a beloved book, a collection of essays titled *The Little Virtues*, by the Italian writer Natalia Ginzburg, and the pages are not only underlined but also bristle with yellow Post-its. Ever since 1990, when I discovered the paperback edition translated into English, I've dipped into it regularly for inspiration. One of my favorite essays in the book (though at one time or another, they've all been my favorites) is "He and I." The opening lines are "He always feels hot. I always feel cold."

Then in a tone of self-deprecation and dry wit, along with great affection, she goes on to compare all the ways in which she and her husband are different — he loves museums, and she goes only when forced; he loves theater, painting, and music, while she loves and understands only poetry; she lists his favorite foods and hers.

"He often says I don't understand anything about food, that I am like a great strong fat friar — one of those friars who devour soup made from greens in the darkness of their monasteries; but he, oh he is refined and has a sensitive palate." Through this device, bouncing back and forth between what he likes and what she does or doesn't like, there's a clear portrait of a marriage between two very real and likable people.

We learn from other writers, and I've learned a great deal from Ginzburg. I stole the setup of "He and I" for an essay I wrote about buying a new house — the first paragraph of my essay is about what my husband likes and what I like in a house. Though rather than *steal*, I like the idea of *borrowing* literary devices we discover from other writers. It's how we learn to write.

TO DO: Think of someone with whom you have a very close relationship. Write four hundred words starting with: *He/she is always . . . I am always . . .* Go into food and art, clothes, houses — all the subjects you don't agree on.

RANDOM ACTS OF LATTE VIOLENCE

One evening a student told me this story about why she'd been late for class: She had gotten out of her car at a red light on Wilshire Boulevard to help an old lady with a walker cross the street in time to make the light. A concerned driver right behind Amy covered her. But just as they reached the curb the light changed, and they were almost knocked down by a driver speeding through the intersection in a huge black SUV with a bumper sticker proclaiming random acts of kindness. Amy, my student, was so angry that she jumped into her car and chased the driver, not knowing what she would do when she caught up with him. She spotted him at a red light, pulled up next to him, grabbed what was left of her latte, and hurled it at him through his open window. She had been so upset she almost didn't come to class at all, she said.

Amy had just gone through the perfect personal essay experience. It had everything: emotion and action, good guys and bad guys. She wrote some sloppy first drafts and read them aloud, taking notes on the feedback she got from the class. The logistics of the story — what car was where when — were hard to nail down, and in early drafts she tended to explain too much. Also, because the situation had made her so angry, the piece didn't have the natural wry tone that her other essays had. While a great story, this one wasn't written in her own voice yet.

After the course was over, she kept working on it, and one day she emailed me about her struggle with the essay: "It was frustrating, and I had to let go of the judgments along the way about my worth as a writer and get back to the basic thing of just telling the story. This kept me on track and worked for my process. I remember thinking, *Oh, this is my process.* I didn't know I had a process. I also realized I had a point with it! Following my own story led me to the truth of the essay and the essence of it — kind of mind-boggling in a way because I didn't expect it."

Her new ending read:

> I've often thought of that man since that day and I wonder if he ever thinks of me. I hope his leather seats got stained from the latte I threw into his car. I hope his wife asked him what the stains were all over the seats. I hope he thinks twice before speeding through an intersection. Mostly, I hope that the next time an old lady tries to cross the street and she can't make it in time to suit everybody's schedule, that there is another person in this city who will look in their side mirror, get coverage from a willing accomplice, and take time out to help her to safety.

It's a good ending — heartfelt, straightforward, and it has a point, even a message. Most important, Amy stuck with it and didn't get discouraged. And she got it published.

Some essays fall into place right away; others can take months to find the shape and the ending. And a paradox: you need to let the emotion cool off to make a piece truly heartfelt.

TO DO: What injustice or rudeness has made you mad recently? Did you do anything about it, or did you fantasize afterward about what you wished you'd done? Write for five minutes.

45

More often than not, endings are hard-won. Usually time solves the problem.

I wrote an essay once about receiving my driver's license with a new photograph. I'd recently gotten a speeding ticket, so my license was not automatically renewed as it had been for the past ten years. I was not happy with this new photograph; I believed it resembled an aging relative of another generation. Trivial as my vanity might be as a subject, I figured other people might identify with it.

So I wrote about my theory, which is that you can use your old, out-of-date license, featuring a photograph of a younger version of yourself, for almost all of the times you're asked for identification, and how this backfired on me in a rather public way in a car rental agency. But the embarrassing backfire wasn't an ending to the piece. It was an anecdote. How could I end this essay about my own vanity? I couldn't. There wasn't any place to go with it. Frustrated, I filed the unfinished essay away under ESSAYS TO WORK ON. And then one night I was watching the news, and a commercial for Grecian Formula came on. A cop stopped someone for speeding, and when he looked at the guy's license and photo, he said, "Why, this can't be you — this is some older fellow!"

There it was — the ending of my essay. When I was stopped for speeding, no cop ever looked at my license and said, "Why, this can't be you — it's some older person!"

The point of this is that your ending can come from strange and unlikely places, even television commercials. Just be alert and patient. And don't hesitate to reveal your own quirks and less-than-admirable obsessions.

TO DO: Write a list of your obsessions and the really petty hang-ups you have. Is there an essay in one of them?

It may seem premature to bring up publishing this early in the book, but the fact is that a personal essay is the most publishable form of creative writing. There's a large market for personal essays in newspapers and magazines, and it doesn't require an agent or writing credentials or a résumé or anybody's approval for you to submit your work. All it takes is a little market research and some knowledge of the basics of submitting a manuscript.

Your essay is a way to connect to the world and have a voice. Okay, maybe you're not writing with getting published in mind; maybe you're writing for therapy or to leave stories for your kids or just for the love of writing itself and as a way to express yourself. And that's fine. As J. D. Salinger said, "There is marvelous peace in not being published."

Sometimes my students act as if it would be unseemly to want to get their work published, just tacky, ego-driven behavior. Or they say it doesn't matter to them, or it would embarrass them, or they're not ready, or any number of dodges. Mainly, they're scared of being rejected. And who isn't? You slave over an essay, pour out your heart, your past, your thoughts, then spend hard hours editing it, and send it off to busy strangers who may or may not like it. It's so much safer not to put your fantasies of being a published writer to the test.

On the other hand, if you want to be a published writer, this is the best first step, because if you have a solid essay and you find the right magazine or newspaper to submit to, you've got a really good shot at being published. I've had whole classrooms full of people roll their eyes at me when I say that. But it's true, and many of those eye rollers now have published essays to prove my point.

A good place to start sending your essays is to your own hometown publications. Just about every neighborhood has a free paper or magazine — check yours for a possible space for an essay. Get a copy of *Writer's Market* or *The Writer's Handbook*. Both books list markets for anything you could write, and have excellent advice on how to submit manuscripts. Go to the library and read current magazines and newspapers. Pick up free publications at your health club. Read the specialized professional publications for your work and see if your writing would fit in. Check out airline magazines when you travel, animal publications at the veterinarian's, child care and health magazines at the doctor's office.

Go to the websites of magazines or newspapers you find that might be a good fit for your writing, and email an editor about writer's guidelines. *The Christian Science Monitor* has such detailed guidelines for its Home Forum essays that it's like getting a minicourse in how to write an essay. Be sure to find out how the publication wants an essay submitted — by regular mail, fax, attachment email, or cut-and-paste email — and if it accepts multiple submissions (that is, essays that have been sent to more than one publication at a time).

When you submit your essay, include a very brief cover letter. If you have a field of expertise that's pertinent to the essay, you might mention that. But basically you're just saying, *Enclosed (or attached) please find my essay (title)* — and then something polite like, *I look forward to hearing from you at your earliest convenience.* If you send it by regular mail, you'll include a self-addressed, stamped envelope (referred to as an SASE in market lists).

Be prepared for rejections. I personally have received enough rejection slips to paper the walls of my office. But realize what good company we're in. There's a long list of masterpieces and bestsellers that at one time were rejected: *Madame Bovary* was turned down by a publisher who wrote to Flaubert, "You have buried your novel underneath a heap of details which are well done but utterly superfluous." *The Diary of Anne Frank* was rejected by a publisher who believed that it "didn't have a special perception or feeling which would lift that book above the 'curiosity' level." Dr. Seuss's *And to Think That I Saw It on Mulberry Street* was rejected as being "too different from other juveniles on the market to warrant its selling."

My favorite rejection story, scary as it may be, is about a novel by Jerzy Kosinski called *Steps* that won the National Book Award in 1969. In the mid-seventies Chuck Ross, a freelance writer, typed out *Steps* and submitted it under the name of Erik Demos to test his theory that new writers don't have much of a chance. Fourteen publishers and thirteen literary agents rejected this National Book Award winner.

—⁂—

The important thing when sending out a personal essay is to know where you'll send it next if it comes back. And I mean have the envelope already addressed and stamped sitting there on your desk, ready to go. Or the next email address you're going to send it to taped to your computer. Because if your essay is rejected, you'll want to race outside and bury it in the backyard.

Instead, pull the arrows out of your heart and stay calm. Read it over and see if there's anything you want to revise (and don't be too hasty — work is rejected for all kinds of reasons: maybe they just published something similar, or, if you haven't done your homework, it's not the right length/subject/tone for their publication). And then pop your essay in the addressed and stamped envelope and mail it, or send it off into cyberspace. Again and again.

Usually newspapers will get right back to you, or their guidelines will let you know that if you don't hear from them in X number of weeks, it's a rejection. Sometimes there's echoing silence for months after you submit an essay, especially to magazines. After two months, write or email the editor a polite note stating on what date you sent the piece and asking if it's still under consideration.

—⁓—

Though it's wonderful to be published, to have your voice out there connecting with the rest of the world and so forth, there is a sobering reality to getting published.

I flew on United Airlines to Denver the month that an essay I'd written about my mother appeared in *Hemisphere*, United's in-flight magazine. I had this fantasy: Everyone on the plane would be reading my essay. Some would be in tears. The person sitting next to me would definitely be all choked up. Then with great modesty I would introduce myself as the essay's author. Word would spread quickly throughout the plane. And by the time we reached Denver I'd be famous as the author of everyone's favorite essay, on page 68.

The reality was that maybe two people on the entire airplane even opened the magazine, and they were not reading my essay. The person next to me was asleep. This is a lesson you learn over and over when you're published. The word *published* means "to make public." It doesn't mean that anyone's going to read it.

TO DO: Make a list of possible markets for your essay, and look up the publications on the Internet. Email for guidelines.

SPEAKING YOUR MIND

There are other forms of short personal nonfiction besides the personal essay, and sometimes the line defining them is so thin that definitions can make you crazy. In brief, these are some of the close cousins to the personal essay:

- Articles written in the first person that include the author's own experiences and opinions
- Columns (weekly or monthly)
- Op-ed essays
- Letters to the editor

A FIRST-PERSON ARTICLE imparts some kind of knowledge, intellectual or practical, to the reader, like a new perspective on South American trade relations or how to build a birdhouse. The author's experience is combined with outside research and interviews. It's also timely. Often travel and food articles are written in the first person and include not only the author's personal experience but also memories and opinions.

Fifteen years ago in an adult-education class I was teaching, a student named Kathy came up with the idea of writing a long list of all the things she knew how to do — everything from writing great memos to making a killer green chili stew. Then she started writing articles about each item on her list. She sold most of them and then sold her idea of the list to a writer's magazine. A few weeks ago I read a "My Turn" essay in *Newsweek* that was very well written. I checked the byline. It was Kathy, as tenacious and disciplined as ever.

TO DO: Kathy's list — write down all the things you know how to do and love to do. Choose one and write a short article in the first person about it.

A COLUMN is ongoing — weekly or monthly, usually — and written in the first person. It can be about politics, fitness, the arts, food, travel, humor, local color, collecting, or just about anything that enough people are interested in.

When I started writing I went to a very small local paper and suggested a poetry column; people could send in poems to me, and I'd choose the ones to be published. Maybe it helped that the editor in chief was the son of one of my close friends, but I instantly got the position of poetry editor. Last spring in class after a discussion of writing columns, three students went out and got themselves gigs as columnists — Beverly for film and theater, Jill as a restaurant critic, and Ted covering yoga and fitness. All the papers they write for are local — no one's making much money, if any — but they have the opportunity to write about something they love, something that's vital in their lives, and to get it published.

AN OP-ED ESSAY (*op-ed* means opposite the editorial page in the newspaper) is usually written by an expert on a subject and encompasses a broader view than a personal essay. Depending on the subject, the "expert" can be anyone from a nuclear physicist to someone who has simply paid deep attention to some aspect of current contemporary life that's in the news. Whoever the expert, he or she has a strong opinion. In class Patty writes about a billboard she finds obscene that she has to drive past every day with her young children, Art writes about being one beer away from the binge that could kill him, Linda writes about giving and receiving too much stuff over the holidays and how to contribute to charities instead, and Elizabeth writes about the power trip of SUVs. All these essays began as personal essays but were published on op-ed pages.

A LETTER TO THE EDITOR can be more than just a cranky rant. In 1994, Linzi, who was born in South Africa, had a letter published in the *Los Angeles Times* when Nelson Mandela became president. Her letter begins with a memory of being eleven years old, standing on a beach in Cape Town. Her father pointed across the water to Robben Island and told her about a brave black political prisoner, Nelson Mandela, who would probably be imprisoned there for the rest of his life. In the sand, she built a prison with a moat around it and marked an *X* where she imagined Mandela to be.

At the end of the letter Linzi writes of recently going to the South African consulate in Los Angeles with her father and her five-year-old daughter to vote:

> My vision of him was no longer vague across a misty horizon, but now clearly in front of me on the historic ballot sheet that had been handed to me.... On it was a picture of Mandela's smiling face, and in the assigned space, I marked, not with a stick in the sand, but with a pen, an X for him.

The letter, only three paragraphs long, is a perfect miniature personal essay.

My father wrote a lot of letters to a lot of editors. Once he called the principal of my school "the little caesar of the educational system" because Mr. Moyer wouldn't mandate that all students learn cursive writing. It was such a dramatic letter that it transcended the op-ed page and was published on the front page of our local Westchester County paper, the *Citizen Register*. My mother was so embarrassed that she refused to leave the house for days.

My father never let up. When he was in his mid-eighties, living in East Hampton, New York, he was back berating the local school board, condemning local nuclear power companies, and airing his views in the *East Hampton Star*. My mother called me once to say his letters had so publicly insulted everyone she knew that she couldn't set foot in the village, and why did my father love to make trouble?

My father, who was simply writing what was on his mind, delighted in the power of his letters to upset people or win them to his side. When he visited me in California he would write letters to the *Los Angeles Times* about trucks going too fast on freeway off-ramps, or rock stars making a mess out of "The Star-Spangled Banner" at baseball games.

I have a scrapbook he put together of all his published letters. Someday I'll give it to his great-grandchildren, with the hope that they'll continue the family tradition of speaking your mind on the page no matter who gets embarrassed.

TO DO: Find something in the news or in your town that you feel strongly about — traffic situations, political stuff, trash, transportation, manners — anything that bugs you or that you feel optimistic about, and write a short op-ed piece or a letter to the editor about it.

3

MEMOIR AND AUTOBIOGRAPHY

WRITING YOUR OWN HISTORY

The way we tell our life story
is the way we begin to live our life.

— MAUREEN MURDOCK

The memoirist, like the poet and the novelist, must engage
with the world, because engagement makes experience, experience makes wisdom, and finally it's the wisdom — or
rather the movement toward it — that counts.

— VIVIAN GORNICK

Writing an autobiography and making
a spiritual will are practically the same.

— SHOLEM ALEICHEM

A memoir relates a journey you took through a difficult time in your life, when things didn't work out or when you were scared to death. When someone you adored died, or when someone you didn't adore died and left you to sort out the guilt, or when you lost your job, or when you turned to religion or got sober, or when you had an accident or a terrible illness, or when you left home for the unknown, or when someone you loved left you. This is not to say that you can't include humor and happiness. In memoir, like life, terrible things occur, and then stretches of the ordinary, and then moments of grace and joy. But a memoir of just grace and joy tends to rot your reader's teeth. No one wants to read about your perfect life unless you walked over burning coals to get there. Humor yes, perfection no.

What keeps memoir from being a long, slow gaze at your own belly button is that the experience is crafted by language and structure, and you came out on the other side. You didn't stay stuck in that period of your life; you moved on — either literally or figuratively, in your head and heart or in concrete ways. You learned something in your experience that the reader can connect to. As Vivian Gornick says, it's the movement toward wisdom that counts.

The memoir, more than any other form of writing, takes a difficult personal experience and shapes it into some kind of meaning. All forms of creative writing do this to some extent, of course, but fiction and poetry wear more veils and masks than the memoir. The memoir is your experience, your truth, pretty much naked.

The best memoir reads like a good story — the author's

experience shaped into dramatic form that creates a powerful experience for the reader. We read to figure out how to live our own lives. Or how to deal with them or find humor. We read to know, as C. S. Lewis said, that we're not alone.

William Zinsser made this distinction between memoir and autobiography: "Unlike autobiography, which moves in a dutiful line from birth to fame, omitting nothing significant, memoir assumes the life and ignores most of it. The writer of a memoir takes us back to a corner of his or her life that was unusually vivid or intense.... By narrowing the lens, the writer achieves a focus that isn't possible in autobiography; memoir is a window into a life."

Remember, it's a window into just one corner of your life, not your whole life.

TO DO: Write about an uncomfortable or difficult corner of your life. Whatever comes to you — images, lists of moments, people, places, dialogue. Let it be as messy as it needs to be. Let it be whiny or bitchy or any way it comes to you.

A MEMOIR IS NOT A HOUSE

But what is the structure of a memoir? my students ask, frustrated with the bits and pieces they're writing.

They want a blueprint — they want me to say, *This is how you write it: place that memory of your thirteenth birthday in the basement and then what happened in Spain on your next birthday as the staircase to the first floor, and on up to the attic with neatly structured experiences, until, voilà! You'll have a memoir.*

While structure is vital, there's no blueprint; each memoir is different.

In the opening pages of *The Disappearance*, a heartbreaking memoir about the death of her two young daughters in an auto accident, Geneviève Jurgensen tells of searching eight years for a way to write her story. Writing was solitary, and she had never worked alone; she was a journalist. Finally she realized that when she talked about her lost daughters she could feel people listening attentively, and this realization led her to structure her story as a series of letters to one of her listeners. She writes in her introduction: "He was close enough (we had met him eight years earlier), and distanced enough (we had not known him when we still had our first two daughters) and he was happy to be sent these letters."

Linda St. John wrote *Even Dogs Go Home to Die* in a scattershot of short disconnected chapters without an ongoing narrative. Some of her chapters are just one paragraph, and none is longer than a page and a half. Each chapter has a title, such as "She Didn't Even Know What P.T.A. Stood For," "Lost Molar," and "They Come by That Meanness Honestly."

Her book opens with her father in the hospital: " 'I don't

want nobody cuttin' on my head,' he kept sayin'. He went on like that for several days. Finally we convinced him he had to have surgery." And then she loops back through her memories of growing up poor with her crazy father and indifferent mother, and returns to his death and funeral, ending with a memory of riding with her father when he was driving drunk: " 'You missed him by an inch,' I cry out looking at dad. 'Inch is as good as a mile,' he laughs. 'Inch is as good as a mile.' " The structure of this memoir — the short snapshot chapters, the rough-edged writing, the pace, the voice — is integral to the story itself.

Don J. Snyder's memoir about losing his job as an English professor and his downward spiral into unemployment, *The Cliff Walk*, reads more like a novel. It begins in the present: he's become a carpenter and has come to terms with his new life as a construction worker; he's found peace. The first chapter is a scene that introduces the setting (the coast of Maine), the rich older woman he's working for, and his past struggles ("I told her the truth about myself then: that like a lot of people in this country I had lost my job and all my money and everything else that I'd always believed added up to the promise of a secure life") and the fact that he's married and has four children. The next chapter begins at the beginning: getting fired.

In *The Color of Water* James McBride tells the story of his white Jewish mother who had twelve black children (who all went on to get advanced degrees), in his own words and also by recording his mother's words: "I'm dead. You want to talk about my family and here I been dead to them for fifty years. Leave me alone. Don't bother me. . . . Hurry up and get this interview over with, I want to watch *Dallas*." But he gets her to go on, and her narrative and his are intertwined to tell the story of her life.

Joan Didion's *The Year of Magical Thinking*, which is as close to pure art as a memoir can get, begins with the first words she wrote days after her husband, John Gregory Dunne, died:

> Life changes fast.
> Life changes in the instant.
> You sit down to dinner and life as you know it ends.
> The question of self-pity.

The lines are repeated throughout the book like a refrain in a poem. In a talk at the Hammer Museum in Los Angeles when the book was published, Didion said that she hadn't wanted the book to be structured; she had wanted it to be raw like grief itself, obsessive and unresolved.

TO DO: In *Encyclopedia of an Ordinary Life* Amy Krouse Rosenthal writes, "I have not survived against all odds. I have not lived to tell. I have not witnessed the extraordinary. This is my story." The book consists of short takes on her immediate life under alphabetized headings. Under "B for Brother" she writes, "My brother, who grew up with three sisters, was I won't say how many years old when he finally realized that he did not have to wrap the towel around his chest when he came out of the shower." Write out the alphabet of your life. A: What's the first thing that comes to you that starts with the letter *A*? Quickly — what word pops into your head with each letter of the alphabet?

BAD NEWS/GOOD MATERIAL

Life handed me a memoir once, though I didn't recognize this fact until two years later. At the time it was just an awful experience arriving at an incredibly inopportune moment — Valentine's Day and exactly six months before my second wedding. But when I looked back at all this two years later, I realized the experience had a very tight, almost perfect narrative frame spanning six months, with a clear-cut beginning, a middle, and then a happy ending — the wedding.

I found out I had breast cancer on Valentine's Day. I couldn't even write about it in my journal the first few weeks; I just jotted down notes on tiny scraps of paper. During my treatment I attended the Wellness Community (a miraculous place, where anyone dealing with cancer can get free psychological support), and when I recovered and my treatment was over, I wanted to give back. So I volunteered to start a writing workshop.

To get people writing about their feelings, I'd talk a little bit about my own experience — the shock of finding out I wasn't the paragon of health I'd believed myself to be, the fears and terrors of 3:00 AM, the frustrations of dealing with the medical establishment, and so on — and then I'd read them poems or quotes from memoirs on these subjects by writers who'd been ill or injured. Amazing writing came out of this workshop, both serious and funny, and I realized that with the workshop participants' writing and the quotes and excerpts I'd found, I had a wealth of material. It had to become a book.

I struggled off and on for about a year with the idea but couldn't get it to come together. I couldn't find the structure or voice for it.

The structure, of course, had been staring me in the face all the time. It was the structure of the workshop itself: talking about my own story, reading the quotes, and from the quotes came ideas for writing exercises, then everyone writing for five minutes and reading aloud what they'd written. This needed to be the structure of my book; I had to include my own story, which would provide a narrative, an engine to drive the book forward.

But it was a really personal story, and I didn't want to go back to that scary corner of my life. I couldn't make it as neat and contained as a personal essay, or layered and veiled like poems or fiction; it had to be what really happened, all of it. The weeping fits, losing my temper, the fears, not feeling sexy, and sometimes having a really lousy attitude.

Finally, with huge misgivings, I began to write it from the very beginning, and lo and behold, my story flowed. Now I'm here to tell you I am not normally a person whose writing flows. Essays, stories, poems — they drip, they trickle from my computer, they waver off in the wrong direction, and they eventually arrive with much wringing of hands and moaning. But writing the truth about the six months before my wedding was like taking dictation. I also discovered humor in my story. And here's the paradox of writing about a bad time: by claiming your story, revisiting it, writing it out, you can also let go of it.

I discovered the tone, my voice for this book, by going back to all those little notes I'd made the first few weeks. I found some that I'd scribbled down in the very beginning — sitting in the waiting room before my mammogram, writing down what other women were doing, what the room looked like, and how sure I was that the lump I wanted to have checked meant nothing. I used the notes I wrote in the waiting room verbatim as the first chapter.

Voice and tone, as well as structure, come out during the writing — unless you're amazingly logical and can sort out all this in your head. Most writers can't. We write to figure out what we're thinking. And only by writing do we figure out what works and what doesn't.

TO DO: Look at that long, sloppy list you made about a hard time in your life. Think of one moment during that time. Pretend you're looking through a window into that moment. Listen for the words; let the smells and the colors come back to you. Feel the sun or the rain on your bare arms, or the rough wool of a blanket. Or the chill of a doctor's office. Look for touch and texture. And write about this one moment. Start with just one word, and then one moment, and then another.

Once you've launched into your memoir, a paralyzing thought may occur to you: *My mother (my kid, everyone I went to high school with . . .) is going to read this.* Yes, this is daunting, and it's tempting to soften details, to cast a fuzz of twinkly light over the whole thing like a Thomas Kinkade painting. Or give up until everybody dies.

There are all kinds of sticky issues involved in writing a memoir — other people's privacy, secrets that could implode entire families, people near and dear to you who may never speak to you again. But remember, you own your story, this is your version of things, and you need to find a way to write it truthfully to the best of your ability.

In her memoir *Breaking Clean*, Judy Blunt tells her story of growing up in eastern Montana before escaping to become a writer. (She wrote the opening chapter as an essay in *four hours*, and it got her a hefty advance for the book, but the book itself took her *ten years* to write.) She wrote of an arranged, loveless marriage: "John had presented my father with a bottle of whiskey and was asking Dad's permission to marry me. I wanted [my mother] to grab my cold hand and tell me how to run." And isolation: "a county so harsh and wild and distant that it must grow its own replacements, as it grows its own food, or it will die."

In a *New York Times* profile when the book was published, a reporter talked to her ex-husband who said he'd read just the reviews, not the book itself, and was "shell-shocked," and that "a lot of people in this county are disturbed." All her mother would say about the book was, "Judy sure has a way with words."

Whatever you write, someone will be disturbed, possibly even shell-shocked.

You have to make your own boundaries. Long ago I decided I wouldn't write personal things about my children. They didn't sign up to have a mother who tells all in print. However, my second husband knew full well what he was getting into when he married me and that he'd be one of my favorite true-life characters to write about.

In my memoir, I referred to him using just the initial *R*. I did this partly because that's how I refer to him in my journal, and it felt more natural, and also it seemed to give him the tiniest bit of privacy. My editor in New York suggested very diplomatically that using just an initial for him sounded a bit old-fashioned and maybe I'd want to use his full name.

So I left it up to him.

"Do you want to be called Bob or Robert or R. in this book?" I asked him.

He thought for a moment, and then said, "I want to be called Tom."

He was R. in the book.

My father was crazy about taking family photographs, especially in front of cars. He'd line up my mother, my brother, and me against the side of the car, and if it was springtime he'd make sure that the forsythia bush next to the driveway was included in the picture. Or he'd photograph us in front of trains, planes, lawn mowers, or dishwashers. There was even a series of pictures of my brother seated in front of a manual typewriter. One of my daughters, who has inherited her grandfather's photography gene, is in awe of the brilliant simplicity of his methods, which I never grasped until she pointed it out. "You're in context!" she said. "It places you in time."

If I ever write an autobiography, I'll include the photographs of my brother, my mother, and me looking cranky and overdressed in front of our yellow Chevy, which in springtime matched the forsythia bush.

Writers love to describe photographs — they can give a kind of shorthand to events. Carolyn See begins *Dreaming: Hard Luck and Good Times in America*, her autobiography and family history, with a search through seventy-five years of family photographs and a description of a picture of her Aunt Helen: "The cruelest person I ever knew, dressed up to beat the band." And then her sister Rose, "Already wearing mascara, one of the things that would get her into so much trouble down the line."

In *Firebird*, Mark Doty's memoir of growing up gay in suburbia, he describes the early love between his parents that he sees in a photograph: "She's all of seventeen, and he merely twenty-three; I feel protective toward them, want to keep them right here, in this bright moment in Chattanooga sixty years ago, the flash of the photographer's lamp finding its match in their unmistakable joy."

In her memoir, *The Kiss*, Kathryn Harrison writes of watching her grandmother cutting out pictures of family members she dislikes rather than discarding the whole picture and event: "Often, she cuts out only the heads and leaves the anonymous bodies behind as a reminder of her displeasure, and her ruthlessness."

TO DO: Choose a family photograph and write about what was going on before or after the picture was taken, or whatever you remember of the people in it. Notice what they're wearing, the setting, the body language.

Denise, who is writing a memoir, does this exercise in class, and it turns into a piece that she'll include in her book. She writes about a photograph taken of her as a teenager with her grandfather in May 1970:

> The lack of awareness that had stifled all of us almost makes sense to me now. There's a visual cacophony going on in that small 3 x 5 photograph taken with my own cheap instamatic. . . . One set of drapes is a green on green brocade, and the other set has an art deco pattern with vines of large pink flowers.

She goes on to describe more of the room, the dress she's wearing that she sewed herself and her grandfather's old flannel shirt:

> None of them ever figured out that I was pregnant. And I never figured out that my grandfather's days were numbered,

or that my father's heart was getting ready to explode from the stress of trying to keep his business from going under. I never figured out that my mother quit drinking milk and eating anything but the smallest portion of meat to stretch the grocery budget. There were lots of things that none of us knew about the others then, and it surprises me that so much of the unknown is visible now in one old photograph.

But maybe you want to write the story of your whole life — an autobiography, not just one window into your life but hundreds. Maybe you started and got stuck: *I was born. . .* you began, and off you went on a linear path filled with facts about your life — your parents, your siblings, where you lived, where you went to school, your teachers, your hobbies. Maybe you ran out of steam at around age eight, feeling like you were sinking under the load of all those facts about your life. Suddenly your life seemed awfully long. Or maybe you never began because the task seemed so daunting.

"The autobiographer's problem," Russell Baker says, "is that he knows much too much; he knows the whole iceberg, not just the tip." (On the other hand, Ernest Hemingway said, "I always try to write on the principle of the iceberg. There are seven-eighths of it under water for every part that shows." Icebergs are obviously a popular metaphor with writers.)

So, how do you write the whole iceberg? Or, how do you write just the tip? When I asked a "Writing Your Own History" class to write down why they enrolled in the course, one student wrote, "My goal is to write my family history in half truths . . . or one-sixteenth truths. So much of my early life remains hidden. I seek tools not only to write but also to remember."

Most of our early memories do remain hidden and only come back to us in flashes of images, smells, and sounds. When I try to think of my earliest memories, I remember an apartment on Judson Avenue in Evanston, Illinois. I'm three or four years old, and my mother is scrubbing a floor with ammonia. I ask her about God, and she says that God is everywhere. I remember the apartment, my mother, God, and ammonia. Why did I ask about God? I don't know, but I can see the room suddenly, my mother on her hands and knees, and I can smell that first shocking whiff of ammonia.

From that one moment other memories begin to stir — I'm in front of the same apartment building. I'm throwing a ball across the street so I'll have to cross the street to get it. I'm told never to cross the street, but I figure if my ball is on the other side I have to cross the street to get it. This makes perfect sense to me. I do it over and over, throw the ball across the street and then go get it. It's exciting, cars honk, and then my mother finally sees me through the window, comes racing out, and spanks me, yelling about being in the street. That night she tells my father we have to move to a house with a backyard. And now that first house comes back to me.

I'm just riffing here — finding a memory, nothing dramatic, just one small window into my own life. Another follows behind, and as you write out these memories, you remember more; the act of writing helps you to remember.

TO DO: Where was the first place you remember living? Look through a window into the first kitchen you had. What do you see? Try to find just one concrete detail. A kitchen table? The stove? Who else is in the kitchen? Write a paragraph or two about this.

Margie once brought her mother, Fannie, who was in her mid-eighties, to the writing workshop at the Wellness Community. Fannie wanted to write her autobiography, but she was overwhelmed by all those years of living that she wanted to get down on paper. She didn't know where to begin. The idea of a series of windows into her past got her excited; she felt she could do this. In the years she had left, she wrote over two hundred pages of memories. She told me that as she wrote, names from eighty years ago would pop into her head, and that if she hadn't been writing, she wouldn't have been able to remember the names. When she died, her family told me her autobiography was the greatest treasure she'd left them.

Another window into your autobiography could be opened to grandparents. When I teach "Writing Your Own History," I always include this poem by Norma Almquist, from her book *Plain Sight*, about her grandmother, to inspire people to write about their own grandparents:

Remembering Nettie Rice White, 1876–1951

Dead gallop cross the pasture in my mind,
She rides the black horse bareback, my grandma.
Gray hair flaring, cotton dress pulled high,
she leans along his neck and rakes her toe

down his soft flank. Her grin is young. Her eyes
are too, as brown and slick as stones rubbed on
the bottom of the creek. She's seventy-five.
I won't see her again. She pulls up slow,

we wave and I drive on. She's there behind,
watching me drive toward things she never saw:
the sea, mountains ranged against the sky,
a canyon, layered cities, old bones

of books chewed over. Her life was not like mine.
Her life was just what happened to her — raw,
suds and sweat, clothes lifted to the line,
mouths to feed, both creatures' and her own

crop of children, falling into time
and space just there on that Missouri farm.
Fourteen slipped from her willing body, supine
on the cornhusk mattress where love had sowed

them. She loved them all. The song and rhyme
and nuzzling love she gave them fringed the hard-
worked days that framed her earthbound, hearthbound life.
Dear Grandma, you sopped up life like cornpone

sops up gravy. I thank you for your grit
and joy, for my pleasure in the scent and heft
of what's alive. I feel you riding in my veins,
chasing the wind, barely touching the reins.

TO DO: Write the word *Remembering* at the top of a page and then a grandparent's or great-grandparent's name. Write down everything you remember or know about this person — or wish you knew.

WHAT'S IN A NAME?

Your name is rich with family history and expectations. I had a student once who had a Russian first name, and we all assumed he was Russian. During a name exercise he wrote that he had lived with this assumption all his life, but it was just that his parents had been going through their Russian phase when he was born, and they loved all things Russian. We know about these phases people go through, and many of them now have grown children named Rain, or River, or Moon.

I was named Barbara for reasons I'd rather forget, but in the spirit of full disclosure, here's the story. For days I was "unnamed baby female" at St. Francis Hospital. My parents flirted with the name Miriam after a favorite actress but couldn't decide. Then one afternoon after visiting my mother and unnamed baby female at the hospital, my father stepped into the elevator of the apartment building with some teenage boys. Desperate by now, he asked the teenagers what a popular girl would be called. Apparently, in Evanston, Illinois, that year it was Barbara. My father, with great pride in his ingenuity, loved to tell this tale of how I got my name. But it always annoyed me. "You just wanted a kid who was *popular*?" I'd say to him in disbelief.

If I were to write my autobiography, I might start with this story. It says something about the time I was born (I doubt there was one female infant on the planet named Madison or Mackenzie that year, and today there are very few, if any, babies named Barbara around). It also tells a lot about my family — my father (would he have asked a group of teenage girls what to name my brother so he'd be popular?), and even my mother, whose absence from my father's story was not insignificant.

We're named what we are for a myriad of reasons: simply because parents like the name, or to honor a relative, or to carry on the name, or to go back to their roots, or because it's trendy or presents an image of what they hope their child will become. Whatever your name, it holds a piece of your family history, and your feelings about your name are also part of the story.

TO DO: Write about your first name. Why were you named this? What do you think of your name?

QUILTS, RECIPES, LETTERS, ETC.

In class Mary, a quilter, has structured her autobiography through the quilts she's made. Each quilt, each chapter, is filled with not only her memories but also information and history about quilting. The quilts are windows into her life.

Jean, who just self-published her autobiography, used the states she's lived in as a way to organize her material and as chapter names.

Like a memoir, an autobiography doesn't have to be linear with a narrative structure. It can go from quilt to quilt, state to state, or recipe to recipe, backward and forward in time. Or the history of your life could be told through the cars you've owned, the houses you've lived in, or in an album of photographs with the stories behind the pictures written in.

Your autobiography could be a blog or a website, an online journal about your family's history, with other members of the family checking in and adding their thoughts and memories. If you're older, it could be in the form of ongoing emails that you send your grandchildren, writing one story about your life every day or week or month.

One night in class, Larry, who had been trying to write stories about ships and war, brought in a letter that he'd written to his first grandchild. He began to read it to the class, but then, overcome by emotion, he had to leave the room. I read the rest of the letter, and the whole class was in tears. There was so much pure love and emotion in the letter, and also family history:

> We've checked your family tree, and this is what we've found. You're part American Indian (some of your ancestors were standing on the shore when the others arrived).... If

your great great uncle Rock were here, he would show you
where your relatives drew on the canyon walls. He would
show you the deer in Zion. . . . If your great grandpa Schmidt
were here, he would teach you to build with wood and how
to fix your car. . . . Your mom will teach you Spanish and
your dad will teach you French. . . . Your grandma Schmidt
can't wait to babysit you. . . . We have so many books that
you will never lack one to read.

One thing about this letter that's so moving is the refrain he
uses over and over like a poem: "We are so glad you are here."

National and international events are a vital part of your autobiography, giving context to your life. Think about the events you've lived through via television. And those your parents and grandparents have lived through: Pearl Harbor; the Holocaust; World War II; desegregation; the Bay of Pigs; the assassinations of President Kennedy, Martin Luther King, and Bobby Kennedy; Vietnam; the moon landing; the *Challenger* blowing up. If these events happened before you were born, ask your parents or grandparents questions and write down their observations and thoughts. A personal view of a larger history is precious.

You experienced 9/11. Maybe you were in New York or Washington DC, or maybe you watched on television, but wherever you were, your life was touched by it. Sometimes when an event is so overwhelming, so horrific, it seems as if there are no more words left to describe it. And this is true: everything possible has been written and said about 9/11 — except for your own version of it. Television images are burned into our minds: the towers falling, the billowing smoke. This isn't what we need to write about in our own histories, but rather, where were we, what were we doing, how did we find out?

Another poem I use for inspiration in "Writing Your Own History" is about 9/11. It's by Jeanne Nichols from her book *Running Away from Home and Other Poems*. Notice the simplicity and grace of the writing, and the juxtaposition of ordinary details and of what's to come.

On a Quiet September Day

The quiet morning light shines on the small black table,
once my mother's, and on the silver bowl from my wedding,
and on my grandmother's purple cut-glass paperweight.

 (Now four men are standing in line, waiting
for their bags to go through the security check.)

I move into the bedroom and pull my mother's trousseau
quilt, embroidered with lavender butterflies, smooth on the bed.

(They are boarding the airliner now, moving
quietly into First Class, walking quiet, sitting quiet.)

In the kitchen I put down fresh water and food
for the cat, and then I move again to the faucet
to water the plants.

(The men sit tightly clasped by their safety belts.)

Now I move outdoors, down the deck, to feed
the goldfish. They flash and suck into the surface
for the flakes, winding around the lily pads
below the waterfall.

(The plane taxis, rises into the morning-blue
sky. The young stewardess smiles,
begins to move down the aisle, offering coffee.)

I come indoors to make my coffee. I sit
down to drink slowly and to watch the hummingbirds

flash swift gold, swooping at the feeder, then away
in great free circles, then returning, radiant,
glittering in the sun.

(The men have moved, have seized the
beautiful flashing plane, now head it toward
the high tower, feeding on their dark fuel.)

Now I turn away from the shining morning,
and I turn on the t.v. to watch
this day's news.

TO DO: What were you doing the morning of 9/11? Use the poem as a model for either prose or a poem of your own, using specific details to carry the emotion.

You might ask during periods of less than optimal self-esteem, *Who would be interested in my life story?*

Generations of your family, that's who. One day they'll treasure the story of your life and perhaps be inspired to write their own life stories. But unless you're famous or living with someone famous, or have been involved in an outrageous scandal, or murdered somebody, your autobiography most likely will remain a family affair. It will probably not be published by a major publisher. An autobiography is a labor of love — for truth, for history, for leaving your mark, for family.

An autobiography is also an opportunity to write about your ancestors, to write down memories and what you know of your grandparents and great-grandparents. It's a reason to interview family members of other generations, to look up your roots on the Internet. Though beware: research can become an excuse to not write. Research is fun and exciting, and it *feels* as if you're writing. (You're taking notes, aren't you?) But doing research doesn't require creativity, not the kind it takes to write narrative and descriptions, feelings and thoughts. So, no, it doesn't count as writing.

The novelist and essayist Mona Simpson says, "I'm a real believer in research, but...I think you should write first and *then* do the research."

—∞—

Here's a list of possible questions for your family members of other generations:

1. Where were you born? Who are/were your siblings, parents, and grandparents?
2. What are your most vivid memories of them?
3. What towns did you live in? What were your addresses?
4. What was your first memory? The first place you lived that you remember?
5. What was the best advice your parents ever gave you? The worst?
6. What was your favorite book as a child? Favorite game? Favorite food?
7. Where did you go to school? What was your favorite subject, and why?
8. What did you dream of becoming when you grew up?
9. What do you remember most about being a teenager?
10. Who was the first person you fell in love with?
11. What was the most powerful national/world event in your lifetime? How did you find out about it?
12. What famous people have influenced you the most?
13. Who were your mentors, and what did they teach you?
14. What was your first job? Your favorite job?
15. What is your greatest passion in life? Your greatest accomplishment?
16. What were the hardest moments in your life? Your biggest regret?
17. What are your spiritual beliefs? Are you religious?

18. What modern invention do you believe is most important and/or convenient?
19. What landscapes do you love?
20. What material possessions do you cherish?
21. What is morally most important to you?
22. What is a perfect day?

TO DO: Answer the questions on the list yourself.

DO NOT BURN

An older woman came to my class years ago and told me she had seven grown children and that when they were little she had wanted to be a writer. All she had time to do, though, in those days was to write down her dreams, her thoughts, her feelings, observations, and overheard conversations. She wrote everything on small pieces of paper and kept them in a box under her bed. One day when her mother was visiting, she showed her the box and told her she was going to become a writer. Her mother glanced through the pieces and said, "Who on earth would want to read this stuff?" My student then took the box outside and burned it in the backyard. And it took over thirty years for her to get up the courage to sign up for a writing class and to start writing again.

There are two lessons in this: 1) Do not show your writing to your mother. 2) Do not burn anything you write in a fit of self-doubt or rage.

TO DO: Write one true sentence about your life. If this stops you cold, write one lie about your life.

TO DO: Write your autobiography in three thousand to ten thousand words. This will get you out of the clichéd five-hundred-word version of your own life that you tell strangers or write on résumés. (This exercise comes from Carol Bly's book *The Passionate, Accurate Story*.)

4

AUTOBIOGRAPHICAL FICTION

WRITING LIES AND TRUTH

If you write just what you know or have experienced,
you've got about a book and a half.

— MICHAEL ONDAATJE

Stories are what show up on the page
once you start hitting the keys.

— LARRY McMURTRY

I don't ever write about real people.
Art is supposed to be better than that.
If you want a slice of life, look out the window.

— BARBARA KINGSOLVER

A student once asked me, "What's the difference between fiction and nonfiction?"

I said, "Well of course, fiction is . . ." And stopped. Wasn't it obvious?

But no one had ever asked me this question before. Fiction is made up, and nonfiction is real? That wasn't totally accurate; good fiction is a mix of both truth and imagination, and in writing nonfiction you're remembering reality to the best of your ability and using fictional techniques like dialogue and setting scenes. So how do you define fiction?

"I'll get back to you on that," I said.

That week I happened to be reading a novel by Elizabeth Forsythe Hailey and experienced an amazing gift of serendipity when one of her characters said, "Finally you must free yourself from the facts and create a lie that tells a larger truth." This has been my official definition of fiction ever since.

Making up stuff gives you freedom. Fiction can seduce your subconscious into offering up the deeper truths of your life, and it allows you to write about things you might not touch without all those veils and masks. You can find ideas, insights, and emotions through your characters that you've never acknowledged, maybe didn't even know you had.

The whole point of writing fiction is to free yourself, to tell yourself a story that you didn't know until you began to write. Or if you did know, how it unfolds becomes a surprise. The point is to put on costumes and play "let's pretend." *But I want to write about my life!* you may be saying at this moment. You want to write what you felt, and what *really* happened.

The interesting thing about fiction is that's probably exactly what you'll end up doing, writing the emotional core of what really happened. And it will be even more true the more you pretend you're making it up.

Lorrie Moore calls autobiographical fiction paradoxical, saying that "the proper relationship of a writer to his or her own life is similar to a cook with a cupboard. What that cook makes from what's in the cupboard is not the same thing as what's in the cupboard." Annie Proulx, in an essay about her story "Brokeback Mountain," wrote, "The scraps that feed a story come from many cupboards." (Like icebergs, cupboards are popular with writers.)

A friend told me that her husband was going to write a novel about his college years. He went out and bought a computer, a printer, and a lot of paper, then set himself up a home office and began to write. He wrote twenty pages and stopped. "There's nothing else to say," he told her.

My guess is that he was writing exactly what had happened to him in college and used up what he thought he had in his cupboard: the experience verbatim, went-there-did-that, with no room for his imagination. He didn't have a plot, a story, or characters that he could distance himself from in order to (paradoxically) get inside his own skin.

At the end of one of the most beautiful pieces of fiction ever written, Norman Maclean's *A River Runs through It*, the protagonist's father says to him, "After you have finished your true stories sometime, why don't you make up a story and the people to go with it? Only then will you understand what happened and why. It is those we live with and love and should know who elude us."

TO DO: Take an object from your desk or your pocket. It could be a ring or your watch, anything that has a bit of history for you. Now write down everything you know about this object: Where did you get it? How do you feel about it? What do you do with it? Write for five minutes.

Find another object. This one belongs to BK. Where did BK get it? How does BK feel about it? What does BK use it for? Five minutes. (Ideally, you do this with a partner who gives you the object he or she just wrote about.)

BK is fiction, of course, and there's no blueprint, no way to do it right, no rules. Make stuff up. When we do this in class to illustrate the difference between nonfiction and fiction, the majority of students, once they get into it, find it more fun to write about BK.

CHARACTERS:
WHY THEY'LL THINK YOU'RE CRAZY

Recently I sent the first half of a novel to my agent in New York, and as I slid the pages into the envelope I had this sense of my characters' voices, their clothes, their rooms, and their habits and quirks and emotions — all getting sealed up in the envelope. And there was suddenly silence.

When I asked the post office clerk how long it took Priority Mail to get to New York, she said my envelope would probably get on a plane that night and then take two days for delivery. All night long I thought of my characters on the plane to New York as if they were actually sitting in seats like passengers. It was like putting my kids on a plane for the first time. *Would they be okay? Most of them belonged in Montana; why had I sent them to New York? Were they ready? Would my agent understand them, be kind to them?*

When you spend so much time with these people, your characters, trying to understand them and hear them, helping them to grow and hoping to give them the best of yourself yet letting them make mistakes and get into trouble, it's a feeling very much like being a parent. Especially when, after all this nurturing and attention, they turn into people who astonish you. Yes, they look kind of familiar (your chin, their father's eyes), but where did they get some of their ideas?

It's this sort of thing that drives family and friends to think you're nuts when you're writing fiction.

Alice Walker wrote about her characters refusing to appear when she tried to begin writing *The Color Purple* in New York City. They didn't like tall buildings, they said. So she moved to

San Francisco, but they complained about the hills; they were country folk, they said. Finally she moved to the country in Northern California where they were happy and agreed to appear so she could write about them.

TO DO: Choose a name from the list below:

Nancy Picardie   Gloria Zimmerman

Jon Rockwell   Tiffany Howell

Jewel Jasper   Daniel Wong

Fordam G. Harrington   Angela Geretti

Raymond Foterhausen   Bliss Dobson

Merta Castillo   Sonny Schermer

Jerome Neilson

Write how your character feels about his or her name. Any stories connected with the name? What kind of car does he or she drive? Any pets? Favorite breakfast food? Current love? Deepest secret? Favorite pair of shoes? Happiest/saddest high school memory? Favorite thing to do on Sunday? How does a close friend/relative/lover describe him or her physically? What does he or she want more than anything else in the world? What's in the way?

Relax and write whatever comes to you, no matter how ludicrous.

There is absolutely no logical way to do this exercise. But trust me — if you're meant to write fiction, weird and wonderful details will suddenly appear out of the air for you. The other day in class Valerie read notes about a character who popped up from under the table and walked around the class, jangling her bracelets and fluffing up people's hair. In another class she'd written about Merta Castillo who, she told us, was still living at her house. This is the kind of mind-set you need to write fiction.

To help you trick your subconscious with the lies right from the beginning, you might want to create a protagonist who's physically different from you — fatter, skinnier, taller, shorter, different hair. Maybe give him your house, or maybe she has a version of your job. But make enough differences in this character to free yourself. The more tricks you use to turn people you know (including yourself) into fictional characters, changing details about them in order to distance them, the closer they grow to you and the more real they become. A paradox.

TO DO: Write a scene with your character from the last exercise. Put the character in a setting with another person from the list. Make it a holiday, have the radio or TV on, and give one of them a pet. Each character wants something from the other and is trying to get it.

PLOT: SHE'S NAKED
AND SHE'S RINGING YOUR DOORBELL

Your main character, Jon Rockwell or Bliss Dobson or whoever, wants or needs something. It's that simple. There's no story, energy, or action without this need. Why does Raymond Foterhausen or Gloria Zimmerman want love, acclaim, money, relationship, power, peace, escape, or an answer to the mystery? What is his or her motivation to go after it? What in Sonny Schermer's background has led him to this moment of desperation? What are the stakes for Tiffany Howell in this situation?

Plot is what happens when your character goes after his or her need or want. Conflict is at the heart of plot — what obstacles are in the way? Something happens, and then that causes something else to happen. Plot begins as ordinary life for your character, wonderful or awful, and then something happens. When A happens, it causes B to follow, and then C. And on to a crisis and then a resolution. Plot is cause and effect.

What most of us need when we start writing fiction is a bear at the door, as Jerome Stern calls it in *Making Shapely Fiction*. "Henry, there's a bear at the door." And it's huge and it's trying to get in, so Henry must take action.

Give your character a bear at the door. It doesn't have to be as big as a bear, or as dangerous, but it has to be something — a phone call, a chance encounter, a fight, a naked woman ringing the doorbell — anything that will create drama.

Nothing of course is impossible, but when there's no bear at the door and you instead begin your story with Nancy Picardie or Daniel Wong mulling things over, staring into the distance, remembering and brooding about the past, you could get off to a pretty slow start.

—◊◊◊—

Another pitfall is to write what really happened, using yourself as the main character, and call it fiction simply because you don't want to offend anyone. If you do this, you're likely to get snagged on your own details. Fiction can be emotionally autobiographical and at the same time not factually autobiographical.

Ask yourself, *What if?* and then step into a situation that didn't happen. Or write a true situation that you push to the limits. Think of a time when something awful and messy happened in your life, but you and the other people involved behaved with restraint — or at least no one blew up or got pissy or threw the good china at each other. But when you write about this situation, let all hell break loose. Push and goad these people, including yourself. Think of everybody as characters and let them act badly or crazily or any way that's opposite of their usual way of behaving. Ask yourself what's really at stake in this situation. Let your imagination and emotions take over.

TO DO: Write a scene in which the doorbell rings. Your character answers it and finds a naked person standing outside the door. Don't think; just write for five minutes. (You're not writing the great American novel here; you're just jump-starting your imagination.)

Plot doesn't happen in a vacuum; it takes place in weather, landscapes, buildings, and time. Your characters have houses or trailers or apartments or single rooms or cots in homeless shelters. Objects surround them — lamps and photographs on top of their dressers, empty beer bottles, stoves to cook food on, collections of things they love, magazines, books, souvenirs from high school. They watch plasma screens in media rooms or old television sets with rabbit ears. They listen to radios, CDs, or iPods that provide a sound track to their lives. They drive cars or ride horses or take the bus or a subway in a particular month and year, in a particular state or country.

I think setting should be the most autobiographical element of fiction, and this is what I mean when I tell students to write what they know. Write *where* you know. Or at least where you've visited and have taken notes. To write an authentic setting you need to know what the air smells like, and over what mountain or building the sun rises in the morning and where it sets in the evening. You need to know what the sounds are: traffic or voices from the street below or from the other side of the alley, seagulls calling or cows mooing, or how deep the silence can be. You need to know the rhythm of the town or village or city you're writing about. You need to know what people order in restaurants or from snack carts, or where they shop for groceries and how much things cost. You need to know the names of the trees and flowers, or the shade of gray of the cement. All these details lend authenticity to what you write. Knowing your setting grounds you literally and figuratively in your fiction.

A sense of place is often mentioned in book reviews. This means the writer has connected to the setting in a deep way — a love of landscape of details of life in a town or city, with the ability to authentically depict an era. Or the total antipathy of a place. The writer has some knowledge of not only the physical lay of the land but also how geography connects with the people who live there, the characters in his or her story.

When Michael Cunningham was researching Virginia Woolf's life for his novel *The Hours*, he visited the River Ouse in England where Woolf had drowned herself. He said in an interview that he'd expected a fast-moving river, but instead it was "this brown swatch of water moving sluggishly across the flat green countryside." At the water's edge he picked up the kind of stones that she must have filled her pockets with to weigh herself down, and suddenly he understood the despair that Woolf must have felt that day in 1941 in a way he hadn't before.

In *Making a Literary Life*, Carolyn See writes about a logistical problem she had when working on her novel *Making History*. For complicated plot reasons, she had to have her characters leave a parking lot on the beach near the pier in Santa Monica and turn north on the Pacific Coast Highway. This is physically impossible if you know the lay of the land because there's a two-foot concrete wall to keep you from turning north. She agonized about this for weeks and then finally wrote, "It was almost impossible to turn north onto the highway. The traffic was fierce. But they did."

Before you fool around with traffic direction and other geographic facts, at least know the lay of the land. And then tinker with traffic flow or whatever else to suit your own plot needs.

TO DO: Have two characters eat dinner in a restaurant, bar, or café you know well. Have them discuss what they're eating, the service, the ambiance. Describe the table or bar, other people, the street outside, the smells and sounds of the place. (Here's another great assignment: go there for dinner and take notes.) Now set these same two characters in a restaurant you've never been to in a city you've never visited. Write their conversation about the food and service, and so forth.

THEME: NO NEON SIGNS

Theme is what the story means, what issues the characters address, and the subtext of your story. Anne Tyler said in an interview that she writes a first draft of her novels and then figures out what the theme is. A lot of writers do this. You're driven to write a story, and then after you've written it you discover the theme embedded in your characters and plot. Some themes are more like axioms, core beliefs you have, and other themes are the big questions you're chasing.

On the other hand, I heard Barbara Kingsolver tell an audience at Dutton's Bookstore when she was signing copies of *Pigs in Heaven* that she started with the theme and then found the characters and a plot to embody it.

If you don't have a theme blazing in your head, don't worry about it. You're not looking for a neon sign here with a message that's more like the end of a fable. Write the story and then worry about your theme or what it all means. If you're writing from your heart and soul, your theme will emerge.

In writing theme, says Stephen Minot in *Three Genres*, "The writer's task is to develop one . . . without becoming blatant."

TO DO: Write how the short story or novel you want to write — or some aspect of it — came from your own experience. Now think about the axiom or question that the story explores. Finally, write how the growth of your central character, or the lesson he or she learns, reflects this theme. (This exercise is borrowed from *Writing the Romantic Comedy*, by Billy Mernit.)

WRITING YOUR CAKE AND HAVING IT TOO

The other day in class a student read a piece she called autobiographical fiction. Unlike other things she'd presented in class, it was curiously flat and careful. When I asked her how autobiographical it was, she said the main character was her, and the parents were also real, as well as the setting and plot. The story seemed stuck between the true freedom of fiction and the honesty and reality of memoir. Maybe she could turn the little girl into a boy? I asked. Or change the setting, or lose a parent — anything to trick herself into thinking she was indeed writing fiction, making it up and wearing a mask so she wouldn't feel self-conscious about writing the story. She finally turned the story back into memoir.

It's hard to write your cake and have it too, to write what really, really happened but under the protection of fiction. Often students in fiction classes, when they've read an amazing scene they've written, sing out, "And it really happened!" That's not the point when you're writing fiction. In fact, hearing that it really happened takes the reader out of the reality of the fiction.

TO DO: Write a true scene from your life. In the scene, change your gender or change the setting — if you live in the city, move the proceedings to a rural location, or if you live in the country, switch it to the big city. (You may also learn something about sexual dynamics and the mix of action and setting through this exercise.)

STANDING ON ICE,
JUGGLING FORTY PLATES IN THE WIND

This is how I started writing novels. One night in an apartment building in Arlington, Virginia, my first husband went to throw out the trash in the incinerator room and returned with a stack of paperback novels someone had obviously not wanted but could not bear to toss down the incinerator. The books were gothic novels — a genre of the sixties and a precursor of romance novels. Each cover featured a beautiful young woman looking frightened and fleeing a dark mansion looming above her. I read them all (we had no money and new books were in short supply), and I discovered a formula.

The novels I usually read and loved simply intimidated me. To this day I can't read Virginia Woolf or Colette without thinking I should lay down my pen forever. But gothic novels had a blueprint: beautiful young woman goes to work as a governess or art restorer for a moody but very handsome man who lives in the looming mansion. By the fourth chapter a dead body is found, and the moody man becomes a suspect. The lovely young woman is in life-threatening danger but falling in love with moody guy, who has a tragic secret and of course becomes the hero at the end. It wasn't literature, but it looked easy. I figured I'd knock off a few gothics and then write the novel of my heart.

I was pregnant with my second baby the summer I started writing my first gothic, and by the time I finished the book the baby had entered first grade. It was my first and last gothic. Not only was *A Grave of Sand* rejected by the publishers I sent it to, but the genre itself had gone out of style by the time I finished it.

But nothing you write is ever wasted. I taught myself how to write a novel by writing that book and then rewriting it over and over. I learned things like how to move characters through space. I don't think there are any rules for this, no easy answers. I just read a lot of novels and followed how other writers did it. But first I had to find out what I didn't know by attempting to do it. Handling point of view and using tenses were also lessons I learned. These are two technical elements of fiction that my students also find confusing.

There are no rules to either point of view or tenses (at least there shouldn't be), but the first thing you need to do in your writing is to not confuse the reader. Or yourself. You can write any fancy, weird, off-the-wall thing you want as long as the reader isn't sitting there saying, "Huh?" And unless you're a genius, go light on fancy and too weird.

Point of view means through whose eyes the story is being told. Basically, there are three choices: first person (*I*), third person (*she* or *he*), and omniscient (a godlike view of the proceedings, in which the author lets the reader know what each character is feeling and thinking). There's also second person (using *you* instead of *I*), but stick to third person or first if you're writing fiction for the first time.

To some extent the omniscient point of view went out of style during the twentieth century, and my advice is to stay away from it. Not because of trends or style but because it's so hard to pull off. Read Shirley Hazzard's *The Transit of Venus* to know how beautifully the omniscient point of view can be done in contemporary novels (and also read it for plot — the ending of this novel is brilliant and heart-stopping). Annie Proulx's short story "Brokeback Mountain" also has masterful control of the omniscient point of view, and in *The Hours*, Michael Cunningham does a magical switch from a main character's point of view, Clarissa's, to that of someone she passes on the street. The resulting character description of Clarissa as seen by this other person is nothing less than breathtaking technique.

In first person, only the *I* of the story sees, hears, remembers, smells, feels, thinks, and so forth. New information comes from other characters through dialogue. It's like acting a part; you slip into the character's skin.

There are levels to the third person — limited, subjective, objective — but to keep this simple, try writing the third person as if it's in the first person but you're using *she* or *he* instead of *I*. That way you won't veer into the omniscient and switch points of view to another character's even for an instant.

A perfect example of switching point of view *within* a novel is in an early Anne Tyler novel, *Celestial Navigation*. (This is different from the omniscient point of view because the switch is from chapter to chapter, not within the same scene.) The book begins with two sisters coming home for their mother's funeral — the first thirty-six pages are told from one sister's point of view in the first person. Then the point of view switches to their brother in the third person. Later in the book, Tyler goes into the point of view of a minor character, and the effect is like watching a film with the camera zooming out to show a long shot of a scene.

As for tenses, write in the present time or past; again, just keep it simple. Fiction can be so complicated to write, it's like juggling forty slippery plates all at once in the wind while standing on ice. Simplify as much as you can in the beginning so you can concentrate on what really matters — your characters, setting, and plot.

In class the other day, Sarah, who speaks four languages and has a master's degree, said she couldn't get a grip on tenses in her essay. She's not alone. But there's one way to keep it simple so you don't have to think about it again. Put all verbs, except in dialogue, in the past tense. If the present tense comes easily to you and you don't get snarled in past verb forms, great; put all your current action verbs in the present tense. It can be energetic writing, immediate and in your face. But if you're writing fiction for the first time and tenses are driving you crazy, keep it simple by putting your verbs in the past tense.

TO DO: Take the scene you wrote earlier from the list of character names and write it in a different tense, either present or past. Now write the scene from another character's point of view.

IDEAS: DUCT-TAPED TO CHAIRS

One day, staring out my kitchen window as fog swirled around the cliffs high above the Pacific Ocean, I thought, *What a great way to get rid of a body — drive it off the cliffs in the fog.* And then, *What if an ordinary person, a housewife, had committed the murder and sent the body off the cliff?* Why or how these warped thoughts came to me, I really have no idea. But the idea came and wouldn't go away and became a novel that would finally sell.

There's no formula or timetable for the arrival of ideas. They can be as rare as hen's teeth, or you can go through a period of so many ideas you're dizzy with them.

When ideas do arrive, they come with a whole slew of questions that require you to come up with even more ideas. For instance, in the novel mentioned above, I had to figure out why this housewife was so crazy she'd kill someone and send the body over a cliff. I lived in her neighborhood; I knew the cliffs; I knew the fog that came in every June; I even picked out which house she lived in; so I had the setting down, the bones of the plot (ordinary person commits a murder and tries to cover it up), but I didn't know who she was and what could happen that would cause her to murder somebody. For months I tried to figure this out, and finally I found her motive in the morning paper.

Newspapers are gold mines for ideas. Read the crime section, read letters to the editor, read advice columns. Curiosity is a huge motivation to write fiction; presumably, when you read about a crime or bizarre behavior or someone at the end of his or her rope, you're asking yourself, *Why?* and trying to construct situations and reasons.

Recently I read in the *Los Angeles Times* a report of a woman who became so annoyed with her husband as they were watching TV and drinking (he was playing with his beard) that she got a roll of duct tape, secured him to his chair, and then stabbed him to death. This raises a number of interesting questions for the fiction writer: Why was she so angry? What had he done in the past that the mere act of fiddling with his beard would drive her into such a frenzy? And how come he just sat there and let her duct-tape him to the chair? Were they drunk? What were they watching on TV?

Other stories that appeared in the paper during one month that could hold an idea for a novel's plot:

- A man is missing in San Francisco, and his family and hundreds of his friends are scouring every nook and cranny of the city looking for a trace of him. They've formed a huge network in cyberspace and are using email to stay connected as they search for him.

- A dog that just won a blue ribbon at a dog show in New York escaped from airport baggage handlers and is missing. Dozens of concerned dog lovers are looking for him day and night.

- A young Southern minister is found shot to death in his house. His lovely wife has admitted to shooting him.

- A red Ferrari going north on the Pacific Coast Highway at 160 miles per hour crashed, and the driver fled into a nearby canyon and disappeared.

TO DO: Find three items in the newspaper this week. See what plot you can make of the situations described. Ask yourself, *Why?* and make up the answers.

CHILDREN'S BOOKS:
THE BIGGEST LIE I EVER TOLD

When you write stories for children you don't have to stretch that much to imagine what it's like to be a child. You still have the same feelings no matter what your age or how much therapy you've had.

When I was six years old I told a lie that turned into such a mess and caused me such feelings of humiliation that I've stuck to the path of truthfulness ever since.

In show-and-tell in first grade I announced I had a grown brother and sister who were movie stars (when in fact I had one brother who was still a baby). I thought it was an interesting idea to have these older successful siblings and that it would get me some attention. It did.

Everyone in school (the *whole* school) had questions to ask, and the more questions, the more lies I had to come up with. If kids visited my house and asked where my older brother and my sister were, well, they were in Hollywood working on a movie, and then I'd have to make up the movie. Then I'd have to describe the apartment in the attic where they lived when they came home from Hollywood. It was a nightmare. I didn't know how to end it.

One day my mother came to school, and the teacher remarked on how young she looked to have grown children acting in Hollywood movies. My mother took this fairly calmly, set the record straight with the teacher, and then told me that I had a wonderful imagination but I needed to tell everyone the truth. I can't remember what I did, only that I wanted to die of embarrassment.

I first gave this as a memory to a character in a novel I was writing, a teenage boy who was dealing with lies his parents had told him. But instead of movie star siblings, I gave him an imaginary lion. And then I realized the story also had the makings of a children's book.

In the children's picture book, when Matthew finally has to tell the truth, feeling he's going to die of embarrassment, he comes up with an idea: he writes and draws his lion story in a book and brings it to show-and-tell. He explains to the class that it was a story he was telling them. "You mean you *lied*?" yells out a smart-mouthed girl in the back row. "He's real in my head," says Matthew. And every week he writes another chapter of his book to read to the class. And it's always interesting.

I realized after I wrote it, that this picture book for four to eight year olds is my autobiography; the story of becoming a writer.

TO DO: Write a memory from childhood that has strong emotion in it: anger, love, hate, fear, wanting, embarrassment. Is there a story here that could be translated into a picture book? Or is it part of a memoir or an essay? Or a memory for a fictional character?

5.

POEMS

FOOLING AROUND

Poetry began when somebody walked off a savanna or out
of a cave and looked up at the sky with wonder and said,
"Ah-h-h!" That was the first poem.

— LUCILLE CLIFTON

Poetry is language surprised in the act
of changing into meaning.

— STANLEY KUNITZ

Perfection is achieved, not when there is nothing more to
add, but when there is nothing left to take away.

— ANTOINE DE SAINT-EXUPÉRY

DROPPING MICE INTO POEMS

In his poem "Introduction to Poetry," Billy Collins suggests holding a poem up to light like a slide, or dropping a mouse into it, or feeling its walls for a light switch, or water-skiing across its surface. But all that "they" want to do is to tie up the poem with ropes and torture it "to find out what it really means."

This is why most of us never liked poetry in high school. We never could figure out what the poem really meant. Poetry was like algebra or the formal essay to me; I just couldn't make it add up. Iambic pentameter? Sonnets, villanelles, sestinas? "This is the forest primeval / The murmuring pines and the hemlocks / Bearded with moss, and in garments green"? I was a teenager, and Henry Wadsworth Longfellow and iambs had nothing to do with what I was interested in, and so they made me feel incredibly stupid. But if some teacher had read me Collins's witty poem about dropping mice into a poem to watch them find their way out, or waving to the poet as I water-skied across the poem, *this* would have gotten my attention.

I discovered poetry I could connect to in the first creative writing class I took and loved it so much, became so passionate about it, that not only did I begin to write poems feverishly, but I also decided to volunteer in local grade schools to teach poetry workshops. I became a born-again poet. I drove people crazy. I was the kind of person you avoid because she can talk about only one thing. I taught for a year in my daughters' grade school, and I was their worst nightmare. I was The Poetry Lady. I was coming to their classroom soon. And I was their mother.

I read the kids poems from the *Paris Review*, and poems by Charles Bukowski, T. S. Eliot, Sylvia Plath, Theodore Roethke, Anne Sexton, and all the other poets I loved. I read poems not meant for children but containing accessible and wonderful wild ideas for them: Eve Merriam explaining how to eat a poem, Ronald Koertge writing about Jane wanting Tarzan to get a haircut, Kenneth Fearing proving that a jukebox has no ears.

The kids also wrote poems of their own: 643 of them, one by each child in the school. I loved their poems — the freedom and flights of imagination, the raw energy, the natural metaphors they came up with. I typed all their poems out; commissioned a cover from Gillan, my seven-year-old daughter; and titled the manuscript *I Used to Be a Vegetarian, but Now I'm a Rabbit's Foot*, a line from one of the kid's poems that to this day is a favorite. I made photocopies and sold them for a dollar each to raise money for the PTA. Then one day I looked at all the poems I'd read, and the poems the kids had written, and thought, *I have a book here.*

So, out of driving my family and friends crazy, causing them to think *I* was crazy, spending a year working for free out of obsession and a need to share my love of poetry with kids, not to mention getting a really bad reputation because I refused to do snack shack duty as a Little League mom since I was too busy with the poems — came my first published book.

I tell you this story because I think those of us who dream of becoming writers need all the encouragement we can get to be crazy, obsessed, and selfish so we can get our writing done. Life is full of choices; think twice before you become snack shack mom or dad if you want to be a writer. You can't do it all. Sometimes you just have to stay home and write.

TO DO: Where is your creativity? Where are your poems (or essays or novels) hiding? Write for five minutes.

I always read a poem at the beginning of every class I teach no matter what the subject of the course. I often get beady-eyed looks from students who signed up for writing fiction or personal essays, not poetry, who think this is some kind of trick, but when I tell them there's no test, no questions afterward about what it means, that it's just a few minutes of their time and attention, they relax. If they love the poem, fine. If not, so what?

But what usually happens after hearing a number of poems is that they begin to recognize that poetry cuts to the chase. Poetry can mainline emotion. Read or listen to a good poem, and you begin to realize the weight of a single word, the power of metaphor, the glorious rhythm and possibilities of language.

We read Jane Kenyon's brilliant and brief six-line poem, "Not Writing," which is pure metaphor: a wasp "daubing" at its nest "but seems unable to enter its own house." I always read this twice in class, first without and then with the title. Without the title you think it's a good image, nice spare use of language; but the title transforms it into metaphor, giving the six lines enormous power, especially to those of us writers who can identify with it.

Thomas Lynch writes of dreaming about his dead parents in his poem "Kisses." In language clear as prose but in the concentrated imagery of poetry, he describes a dream: his father on roller skates wearing wing-tip shoes, the hope that maybe he's not dead after all, his mother having gone on ahead to make coffee after the movies, and his father saying, "He'll take my kisses home to her."

In "Valentine for Ernest Mann," Naomi Shihab Nye tells

about someone asking her to write a poem for him. "You can't order a poem like a taco," she replies in the poem. But she's writing one anyway, telling a story about a man who gave his wife skunks for Valentine's Day and couldn't understand why she wasn't happy. "He was a serious man / who lived in a serious way. Nothing was ugly / just because the world said so." She ends with the idea that maybe we'd find poems if we reinvented what life gives us. "Check your garbage, the odd / sock." It's a witty poem with a lovely idea to hold on to.

However, all this spare imagery, dazzling metaphor, and wit can be intimidating when it comes to your own writing, so when we write poems in class I start with Raymond Carver's poem "The Car." Forty-five out of forty-eight lines in this poem start with the words *the car* and offer factual information: the car that didn't have brakes, the car that one of his kids crashed, the car that had a leaking radiator, and so forth. On the surface this looks like a very simple poem — hardly a poem at all, a list in fact — and this offers courage for leaping into writing a poem of your own.

TO DO: Think of an object in your life, a *thing*, not a person or pet or place. It can be as small as a ring or as large as a house. Write about it, starting every line with the object. ("The ring that . . ." or "The house I . . .") You don't have to explain anything; just one thought or observation about this object for each line. Go for five minutes, and don't think.

LOOKING FOR HAIKU

Haiku is a form of Japanese poetry with three lines and seventeen syllables, five in the first and last lines, seven in the second. (Though if you read translated haiku, the syllable count is not always accurate. In Japanese *onji*, sound symbols, not syllables, are counted.) Writing haiku is as much about seeing as it is writing. It's about catching one instant of awareness in a snapshot of words.

Here's an example of haiku by a Japanese master, Yosa Buson:

Walking on dishes
the rat's feet make the music
of shivering cold

Notice how simple it is but what a powerful picture it creates — the rat, his feet on dishes, the cold. Haiku shows rather than tells.

Contemporary haiku often replaces the traditional Japanese focus of nature and seasons with the concerns of the twenty-first century. The following series of haiku by Anonymous (the first funny haiku I'd ever read), circled the Internet:

You step in the stream
but the water has moved on.
This page is not here.

A crash reduces
your expensive computer
to a simple stone.

Three things are certain:
Death, taxes, and lost data.
Guess which has occurred?

Windows NT crashed.
I am the Blue Screen of Death.
No   one   hears   your   screams.

Once I had a student who was taking a course I teach that covers all the different genres of creative writing. But he made it very clear to me that all he wanted to write was his family history. When we came to the poetry and haiku section, he wanted no part of it, but he finally agreed to try just a few haiku for homework. The following week he read them aloud, and the class loved his work. He had a talent for taking word snapshots — simple and eloquent. He kept writing haiku and got published, and then he began to study Japanese so that he could write haiku in traditional forms. It was like introducing someone to the most unlikely blind date and having the person fall madly in love.

TO DO: For one week write a haiku in your journal every day. In the beginning try the 5-7-5 syllable count; it's like having a net to play tennis with (to paraphrase Robert Frost). Your haiku doesn't have to be brilliant. No one will ever see it. But having to write just one haiku a day will cause you to look for it. And looking for haiku can be just as important as writing it.

THE COYOTE IN CENTRAL PARK:
FOUND POEMS

Found poems are exactly that — poems you find already written. You just have to get rid of all the unnecessary words to ex-
pose the poem. Found poems are, as Annie Dillard says, "editing
at its extreme: writing without composing." You can find poems
in the newspaper; you simply pare away as many words as possible and turn what's left into short lines. Here's a poem I
found in the *New York Times* from a long article by James Barron about a coyote caught in Central Park:

coyote's romp
in Central Park
dip in a chilly pond

helicopters overhead
out-of-breath posse
officials
reporters
    trailing

four acres of boulders
and grass
the carousel
quick swim
across duck pond
past the rink
    where an actress in a wig
    was doing figure eights

Every word came from the article, which began with this paragraph: "A coyote's romp in Central Park ended yesterday with a tranquilizer dart and a nap, but only after a messy breakfast (hold the feathers), a dip in a chilly pond and a sprint past a skating rink-turned-movie set."

Dillard found her poems for *Mornings Like This* in a junior high school English book circa 1926, emergency care manuals, watercolor instructions, and so forth. In *Cugle's Practical Navigation* she found lines decoding flag signals that gained a whole new edginess when written as a poem:

Do not abandon me.
I am undergoing a speed trial.
Keep clear of me — I am maneuvering with difficulty.

Found poems not only are fun to discover, but they also teach you to look at words in a fresh way, to find poems embedded in everyday language, and to realize what words carry weight and how powerful their arrangement on a page can be.

TO DO: Find a poem in a newspaper article. Pare out as many words as possible. Cut the lines any way you wish, but keep the same sequence.

DARK SADDLES OF GREED:
POETRY CONTESTS

One of my students, very excited, called me one morning with news of a heavily advertised poetry contest — huge prizes, no reading fee, and the possibility of being included in an anthology that, according to the ad, was a sold-out, sought-after sourcebook for poetic talent.

The idea of people seeking poetic talent through a sourcebook was bizarre, to say the least. Even the thought of anyone on this planet actually hunting down poets (while a nice idea) was pretty amazing. Add the thousands of dollars offered as prize money, and the whole deal sounded suspect.

I told my student that before she entered her poems we'd investigate the contest by sending in a poem written by the whole class.

We wrote a poem as a group project in five minutes. We had a marvelous time; the poem was terrible. We named it "Estranged Partners," and it included such lines as "Where did you sleep last night? / I slept on her divan." (The guy who came up with the line "I dreamed of dark saddles," however, was rather proud of it.) The class was being held on the UCLA campus, so we used Beverly Glen, a nearby street, as a pen name.

A month or so later we received a letter: "Dear Beverly, It is my pleasure to inform you . . ." We learned that the selection committee had certified our poem as a semifinalist in the contest. Moreover, in view of Beverly Glen's talent, they wanted to publish "Estranged Partners" in their next anthology. The publisher's list price for the anthology was $69.95, but if we ordered it now we could get a special deal for $49.95. For another twenty dollars our biography could be included.

Even acknowledging the huckster quality of the acceptance letter, we thought maybe "Estranged Partners" had been a fluke; we'd had too much fun writing it. We didn't try hard enough. Our poem wasn't *that* bad. (Maybe the line about dark saddles did have a certain weird flair...) The only real test would be to write an aggressively bad poem, a poem so awful that you couldn't read it aloud without flinching.

The following term, we wrote what we all believed to be one of the worst poems ever committed to the English language. It was titled "The Poet's Pen" and opened with the lines "My pen is a vein filled / with blue ink." It went from bad to worse a few lines later with "My pen pulses life's blood. / My pen spurts my emotion / onto the willing paper." We signed ourselves John E. Anderson Jr. in honor of the building the class was held in.

A month later another letter arrived: "Dear John, It is my pleasure to inform you..." This time not only would we be published in the anthology, but for $29.95 (plus $3.00 postage) we could get a professional reading of our poem on tape. Our "artistry" (a direct quote from the letter) would not be recorded without our permission. Also available, for $38.00, was our poem presented on a walnut-finished plaque with two choices of border decoration.

In subsequent classes I've discussed the contest, and there's always at least one embarrassed student (an intelligent, sophisticated adult, serious about writing poems) who has been caught by this scam. Maybe nothing illegal is going on here, but neither is anything remotely connected to poetry. To be told that we had "a rare talent," that the terrible, silly poem we wrote as a class experiment was "a work of art" and "only one of a few chosen from thousands of poems" (the mind boggles at the thought of this possibly being true), and that we should be "genuinely proud of our accomplishment" is a pack of lies at best.

The contest's anthology is published four times a year, and there are thousands of poems in each edition. With poets buying tapes, wall plaques, and copies for their friends and family, plus paying to have their biographies included, it turns out to be a huge moneymaking deal for the people who run the contest.

But at least they drew the line somewhere: neither Beverly Glen nor John E. Anderson Jr. won a cash prize.

6.

YOUR WRITING LIFE

One thing about writing is that it takes time.

— M. F. K. FISHER

If you don't have the time to read, you don't have the time or the tools to write.

— STEPHEN KING

If writing is thinking and discovery and selection and order and meaning, it is also awe and reverence and mystery and magic.

— TONI MORRISON

I'm not very organized about religion; nor do I believe in angels or the levitation of spoons or the possibility of contacting dead loved ones — but I do believe in a spiritual dimension to things. I just don't know how it works. Something's out there, and maybe all that's required of us is that we stay alert. My spiritual messages sometimes come from the muse, and the other morning the muse came in the shape of my painter friend Laura who lives in Arizona. I was stuck with my writing, and I sent her a whiny little email about how I would never finish this novel I was trying to write, and *oh-woe-is-me*. She wrote back something encouraging and then went on to tell me about a piece she was working on, an icon — a religious picture painted on wood (and though it's painted, creating an icon is referred to as "icon writing"):

> I sure hope this icon turns out, but a friend reminded me that the icon is not about ME, and St. Luke will turn out as he pleases. Also, one of the tenets of icon writing is that you never turn back. You can fix a bit, but you just keep moving, and that is exactly the lesson I need to learn on a lot of different levels. I also hear my father's axiom — *the perfect is the enemy of the good*. I don't think that's a cop-out; it's just the same thing as *do your best and keep moving*.

The muse had spoken. I wouldn't turn back. I'd do my best with this damn novel. It wasn't all about me; it was about my characters and their story. I'd keep going and stop whining. I emailed Laura right back and thanked her profusely for such a great metaphor. She replied:

Icon writing is chock-full of interesting metaphor. In some icons the layers of paint underlying all but the skin are called the "chaos" layers... — and it really does look chaotic — darks and lights, blotchy. It adds life to the work. And, like life, chaos is just under the surface.

Chaos layer. Pure gold. The perfect metaphor for writers. We're writing out of chaos; all darks and lights, and blotchy. Not only does our work feel like chaos, but our lives usually do too. We're all trying to subdue the chaos with Palm Pilots and BlackBerrys and to distract ourselves with iPods and the Internet. But it's all chaos, and that's why we write. To make order and meaning out of it. And our first task is to get calm enough to sit in a room all alone with our thoughts and fantasies, and then let our writing get as messy as it needs to be, let the chaos spill out on the page, before we find the order and meaning.

CATCHING THE CAB: RITUALS

In her no-nonsense book on making creativity a habit, the choreographer Twyla Tharp writes about waking up each morning at 5:30, pulling on her workout clothes, and going down to the street to hail a cab to take her to her gym. "The ritual," she says, "is not the stretching and weight training I put my body through each morning at the gym; the ritual is the cab."

The word *ritual* has spiritual connotations — religion and worship, formal and ceremonial. Faith is involved. *If I do that, this will happen. If I drink my coffee in this cup, the words, the dance, the painting, the music will come. If I wear this sweater, the work will go well today.* The main ritual, though, is catching that cab, or putting on running shoes, or sitting down with a pad of paper, or turning on the computer. Choice is taken out of it by making it a ritual.

Writers have many variations to the ritual of beginning to write each day. Julia Alvarez begins with fresh flowers or lighting a candle in her writing room, then fixing strong Dominican coffee that she drinks in the study while reading poems. "This is the first music I hear, the most essential," she says.

Tom Robbins said there are four things that writers should do to get into the writing mode:

1. Thirty minutes of yoga or some physical activity, because writers live too much in their heads. ("You need to be grounded in your physical body.")

2. Another half hour reading poetry or something unrelated to what you're writing.

3. Look at clouds, or a night sky, for half an hour.

4. Think about sex for thirty minutes. ("Get yourself in, not necessarily a frenzied state, but in a state of great intensity.")

In *Life Work* Donald Hall writes of beginning his day reading the *Boston Globe*, eating a blueberry muffin and a peanut butter sandwich and drinking coffee while feeling the "work-excitement building," and then going to his desk at six AM.

I personally would love to place fresh flowers and light candles in my writing room, but this could lead to disaster with Stuart and Charlotte. I'd love to come to my desk every morning filled with work excitement, and sometimes I do, but more often I come with a thousand little gnawing details of life filling my head. As for spending half an hour looking up at the sky and then another half hour just thinking about sex — well, that sounds like fun but, really, who has the time?

But I love to read about the rituals of other writers — to think of Toni Morrison getting up to make a cup of coffee while it's still dark out. "It must be dark," she says in Jill Krementz's *The Writer's Desk*, "and then I drink the coffee and watch the light come.... It's not being *in* the light, it's being there *before it arrives*. It enables me, in some sense." And Carolyn See listening to Van Morrison: "His whispered words buoy me up." And Donald Hall in New Hampshire eating his peanut butter sandwich and blueberry muffin before dawn.

TO DO: What rituals can you come up with for yourself to take the choice out of whether to write today? What place can you find to write in, and what music can you play to help you create what See describes as, "a little hut for your soul with everything it needs ready at hand"? Brainstorm for five minutes.

Where and when you write isn't trivial, and if you take this seriously you'll take your writing seriously too. My first desk was the kitchen table, with my work kept under it in a small portable file. My girls were toddlers then, eleven months apart in age, so I'd write during their nap time, setting the kitchen timer for one hour. The house rule was that unless they were bleeding they could not enter the kitchen and disturb Their Mother Who Was Writing until they heard the timer go off. I made the sanctity of my writing time sound like such a big deal that I convinced not only them to take it seriously; I convinced myself as well.

Over the years and in different houses, I moved out of the kitchen to bedroom desks, and then when my first novel was published with a movie option, I built a room of my own — an office addition to the house. (And then discovered that any construction project is the all-time excuse for not writing.) But the magic has always been in the paper, the computer, the first cup of coffee, and the rush of having a writing project that's going well, or at least going.

You don't need much equipment to become a writer. Just a notebook, a pad of paper, pencils or pens, and eventually a computer. A few CDs or a radio if you want to work with music. And a place that feels private and comfortable to you, a place to keep your work.

In *The Writer's Desk* Jill Krementz photographed William Maxwell writing in his pajamas and robe with a mess of books and papers behind him; Cathleen Schine writing, fully dressed, on her bed; Rita Dove standing, writing at a high, bare desk in her cabin with candles lit; Richard Ford writing by hand on a clipboard, his feet on a child's desk (and quoted saying that he can write in a rental car, on a Greyhound bus, or on a plane: "I carry my desk with me"). There's also a picture of E. B. White sitting on a wooden bench, his typewriter on a plain table, a small antique barrel on the wood floor below, a window to his right, open to a view of water. His space is as spare and elegant and useful as his writing.

TO DO: Decide where you'll write and when. Where are you going to keep your work and tools?

I'VE GOT PAGES AND I'VE GOT A GUN

There was a *New Yorker* cartoon a few years ago with a guy holding a group of people at gunpoint, and the caption read: "Now, I'm not going to hurt anybody. I just want to read you a few pages from my novel." I didn't use a gun, but very recently on a lovely Sunday afternoon in Los Angeles, driving downtown to a concert, I said to my husband, "I just happen to have a few pages here I need you to listen to."

He didn't blink, just kept driving, and I read my pages all the way down the Santa Monica Freeway to the concert.

But other than using a gun, or holding your reader hostage in a moving car, how do you find the person who you can trust with your pages, let alone who is willing to read or listen to them? This is one of the best reasons to take a writing course or to join a group of writers. But only if it's a positive class or group, only if guidelines are set up that will nurture everybody's writing, not tear it apart for the purpose of making someone else look smart. On the other hand, you don't want a bunch of people just telling you everything you write is wonderful, wonderful. You need to find a teacher or a group of people who are there not to talk about themselves or to prove how clever they are but to honor words on a page, language and story, and to discover something worthwhile in those words and then how to make the story even better.

TO DO: Check out creative writing courses offered by local colleges or adult ed programs. Go online to find writing websites that offer inspiration and advice, and look for writing groups in your area.

ONE PERFECT BOWL:
TAKING WRITING COURSES

I once took a ceramics course at a local community college and became obsessed with throwing a perfect bowl on the wheel. I told Jay, the instructor, I didn't want to do any assignments; I just wanted to make this bowl I had in my mind. I was manic about the whole idea. It was a spiritual quest for the only object that you'd need to contain food; a bowl for soup and salad and cereal. It would be beautiful in its simplicity and usefulness. Very Zen. Et cetera. Et cetera. Fortunately, Jay was a true artist, a ceramist and also a painter, and he didn't think I was nuts or feel threatened by my ignoring everything he taught except for this one thing. I wasn't terribly talented at ceramics, but I made hundreds of bowls — early on they each weighed about ten pounds, and to this day they function as dog and cat dishes for my friends' pets. In the end I made maybe six decent bowls, not works of art, mind you, not perfect, but we're still eating cereal out of them.

The point of this is that you're not going to take a writing course or a workshop to become a surgeon or to learn ancient Greek; you don't have to memorize anything or take tests — you're going because a class or workshop will make you take your writing seriously, you'll have deadlines, and maybe you'll learn a few writing guidelines and get constructive feedback on your work. But mainly you're looking to make the perfect bowl, your story. It'll never be perfect, but that's okay. As my friend Laura's father says, the perfect is the enemy of the good. But it's your bowl and your vision. And that's why you're there.

If for any reason a writing teacher makes you feel stupid or embarrassed or untalented, leave immediately; get your money refunded, and don't go back. Life is too short to waste your time on negativity and to endure unnecessary public humiliation. If you have assignments that you hate, that drain your creativity, if you start to lose your desire to write — don't go back. Writing is about taking risks, and you can't take risks if there's the chance of someone making fun of you or being sarcastic. You have to find a safe place to take your writing to. Nothing you ever write will be a waste. It might not work, and a good workshop will let you know this, but you had to write your way through it to get to your best writing.

A writing workshop should be fun as well as work. Here are all these people gathered together who love what you love. They're not after fancy cars or a cover on *People* magazine — these are people who love books and want to write their stories, their truth. No one can be creative if an instructor or other students are tearing one's writing to shreds to boost their own egos.

It takes a lot of courage to come to a writing class and read your work out loud. There's got to be a high level of trust, and the acknowledgment that we're all in the same boat, we're all trying to write an honest story, trying to make sense of our lives. We're all just trying to connect, and this can happen only with a generous heart. So you need to find a place where you can fool around, take risks, and have some fun.

I have a beautiful blue abstract painting hanging in my house, painted by my grandson Axel at age two. I also have a photograph of Axel painting the picture; he's covered in blue paint. It's on his arms and his face and in his hair. When you write, let yourself get into the blue paint. Find yourself a teacher who will let you make a mess. It's only the first step.

A number of my students have gone on to form their own writing groups after leaving class, using the class's format. For each meeting one person is designated the leader. That person brings in a topic for discussion with quotes from books or articles for illustration and inspiration, gives a writing exercise, and then conducts a workshop for feedback on the other members' writing.

If you take a class or decide to start your own workshop, here's some advice for giving feedback:

- Be generous, honest, and specific when you critique someone's work.

- Take notes while listening to the work so you can give detailed feedback.

- Don't veer off into personal comments — stick to the writing.

- Don't try to rewrite the piece for the author; find out his or her intentions.

- Frame your comments with:

  I don't understand . . .
  I want to know more about . . .
  I'm not sure what the point is . . .
  I really liked xyz because . . .
  Xyz made me feel . . .

The writer doesn't respond to comments until everyone has finished giving feedback. When your work is being critiqued, you just take notes on what the group says; otherwise, you'll find yourself trying to defend or explain your work.

Have copies for people to read. They can give much better feedback when they read as well as listen. And I think it's important to read work out loud. As the author, you'll learn more about your writing by hearing little noises or total pin-dropping silence from the others in the workshop as you read. And you'll also pick up the bumpy spots in your writing.

Don't allow people to talk away their stories instead of writing them. It's a *work* shop, not a social hour.

I tell my students they can read an essay about how they became homicidal last night, chopped up their partner, and put the pieces in trash bags in the trunk of their car, and we will not comment on their behavior. We will simply discuss how they wrote about it.

TO DO: Sign up for a workshop or find a friend (or a group of friends) serious about writing and make a commitment to meet once a week or month to read each other's work. Set goals and deadlines together.

THE HOO-HAHS

I read about the hoo-hahs in a quotation by a New York agent in a writers' magazine: "We get a lot of manuscripts with fifty-page hoo-hahs," she said. Remember the bear at the door story? Well, the hoo-hahs mean that the reader has to get through fifty pages of a book before the bear shows up. At the time when I read the quote, I was having problems with my novel, so I immediately called a writer friend and said, "I wonder if my book could possibly have the hoo-hahs."

He laughed and said, "Oh, that's some New York agent just trying to be cute."

And then I asked my friend to read the first hundred pages of my novel to see if he could figure out what the problem was. A few days later I got an email message from him saying, "Yes, you have a problem and I think I know how to fix it." He came over to my house and said, "You need to cut the first fifty pages."

"Are you trying to be cute?" I asked.

He shook his head. "Your story starts on page fifty."

Well, okay, maybe the action does click into gear when my main character actually gets to where she's going on page fifty. But the lead up! All those sweet details about her house and what's planted in her garden and how she feels about her photography and that wonderful stuff about the wedding she shoots at the Bel Air Hotel and the couple's dogs in the ceremony and the little baskets of white flowers around their necks...

My friend was ruthless. "Page fifty," he said.

That's where the bear showed up. That's when the naked lady rang the doorbell.

I know this, of course — I teach it. *Kill your darlings*, I blithely quote to my students. *You write your way into essays and fiction*, I say to them. *You're telling yourself the story, then you throw out first paragraphs, first chapters! Get to that bear right away.* But it's one thing to know it and a whole other thing to see it clearly when you're sitting alone in your room rereading your pages. It's hard to have perspective. Especially when you're in the middle of writing it. A workshop can often give you clear feedback, or sometimes you just need to put it away for a while. Or show it to an honest writer friend.

TO DO: Read your manuscript for the hoo-hahs. As you did in your essay, find where the chase begins and cut to it. But don't tear up your hoo-hahs; don't delete them. Place them carefully in a folder and label it NOTES FOR NOVEL (or NOTES FOR MEMOIR). They'll remind you where you started and why.

There's a second act to my hoo-hah story, which involves another appearance of the muse. A few days later, after I cut my first fifty pages, I was in Trader Joe's buying groceries. As I was reaching for a carton of milk, I ran into another writer friend who asked how my writing was going.

"Billy told me to cut the first *fifty pages* of my novel," I said in a drama-queen tone.

Peter laughed. "Oh, my agent told me the same thing. Cut the warm-up and get to the first pitch." He was so casual about it, so easy about the whole thing.

I lightened up immediately. I felt as if I were suddenly in a community of writers who all shared a slight case of the hoo-hahs. And it was okay.

And it's okay for you too.

IKEA AND SNORING DOGS:
PUBLISHING IN PERSPECTIVE

We think publication will change our life. But it doesn't. There
is of course relief (hey, all those hours sitting around in your slippers weren't for nothing!), and your family is amazed that this
hobby of yours has suddenly paid off (though if you figured out
your hourly wage you might get seriously depressed), and it is
wonderful fun for about fifteen minutes. But getting published
doesn't make it easier to write — in fact, it often makes it harder.

One of my students came to class with a copy of my first
novel and asked me to autograph it. The book was long out of
print, and I asked her where she'd found it.

"It was part of a furniture display at Ikea," she said. "They
had a bookcase filled with books, and I had to talk to the manager before they'd let me buy it." This gave me pause; my first
novel, now sold as books-by-the-yard for decorating purposes.

During a bookstore reading for my last book, from a chapter
I thought was funny in a dark-humor sort of way, I heard a man
in the front row muttering, "Oh, no, so depressing. Oh, dear." I
pretended I didn't hear him. But then I heard snoring. The man
had brought his dog (introduced to me earlier as Mr. Bubba), and
Mr. Bubba had now fallen asleep under the podium and contin-
ued to snore loudly throughout the rest of my reading.

You think the world will stand still in awe when you finally
publish — or even simply finish — your essay or your book.
The truth is, the world will most likely go on shopping at Ikea
or snoring, or doing whatever it needs to do. Possibly it might
be impressed for a second or two. But what's truly important is
that you'll know and your community of writers will know the
struggle you've gone through and what you've accomplished.

One day in class everyone was moaning about how blocked they were and how hard it was to write, questioning whether they were real writers, making excuses why they couldn't do any writing that week, and relating all the not very encouraging things their mother/father/spouse/ex-boyfriend/girlfriend had said about their writing. That night I sat down and wrote the list of pointers that you see on the next page. I handed it out in class the following week.

But why take any of that advice? Why write in the first place? Why not just ignore the ache or the itch to put your life down on paper?

Because if you're drawn to language and books, to stories and poetry, you need to pour your creativity into writing. To live your own true and precious life, you need to express yourself and make your inner life as important and as known as your visible life. Whether you're published or not, you need to turn the chaos and the glimpses of beauty, the questions and the search for answers, the days and months and years of your life into something meaningful on a page.

When you finish a piece of writing, you've reached out to the world with your own truth. You've told your story.

EVERYTHING I HAVE TO TEACH YOU ABOUT WRITING, ON ONE PAGE

1. Here's how you learn to write:

   a. *Read*. You need to be inspired, and you need the very best teachers in the world. You find this by reading.

   b. *Write*. Writing is like running a marathon or playing the clarinet or laying bricks or playing basketball. You need to practice.

2. There's nothing until there's something on the page. If it's just in your head, it's fluff. Once it's on the page, it's real; you have a departure point.

3. Writing is a two-part process. You write and then you edit. You can't do both at the same time. Write your first drafts so fast that you have to get out of your own way. Then let your critic loose and edit.

4. All that's required of your writing is that it's honest and specific. You don't have to get fancy, clever, or literary.

5. The word *write* is a verb. Don't worry if you're a "real writer" or not. You are someone who writes. And you do it every day if you're serious about it.

6. Be careful who you allow to read your writing. Find readers who are nurturing and honest. While you might have a nurturing and honest spouse or partner or parent or grown child or best friend, he or she will not be the best person to read your work. You're a spy in their lives. You're telling the truth.

Acknowledgments

Thank you to:

My teacher, Norma Almquist, who gave me the courage to write and who, with transcendent generosity, still reads my early pages.

My students, each and every one. There would be no book without them.

My early readers (all worth their weight in gold and rubies) who said to keep going: Bill Mattes; Jennie Nash; Jeanne Nichols; Pat Shannon; Jacqueline Winspear; and Billy Mernit, who can make me laugh in the middle of any major writing problem.

My agent, Lisa Erbach Vance, for her belief in this book and her advice, which had a profound influence on it; and Aaron Priest, always.

The dedicated and talented team at New World Library: my editor, Jason Gardner, for his confidence in the book; Paula Dragosh for her copyediting; Kim Corbin and Munro Magruder for their energy and ideas; Tona Pearce Myers for the interior design and typography; Tracy Pitts for the cover design; and especially, Kristen Cashman for her sensitive, smart, and meticulous editing.

Linda Venis, director of the Writers' Program at UCLA Extension, who gave me the job that taught me what I know about teaching writing and who came up with the title of this book as the name for a course. And also her staff for their genius at making writing instructors happy and calm.

Sally Court for once again holding my hand while I wrote the last page.

My beautiful daughters, who managed to survive The Poetry Lady.

My husband, the ever patient, witty, brilliant, and beloved R.

And Emma, Axel, and Grace simply for being on this earth.

PERMISSION ACKNOWLEDGMENTS

The author and publisher wish to thank the following publishers, authors, and publications:

Page 73: Norma Almquist, for permission to use her poem "Remembering Nettie Rice White, 1876–1951," from *Plain Sight*, copyright © 2003 by Norma Almquist.

Page 80: Jeanne Nichols, for permission to use her poem "On a Quiet September Day," from *Running Away from Home*, copyright © 2003 by Jeanne Nichols.

Page 115: BOA Editions, Ltd., for permission to reprint an excerpt from "A Valentine for Ernest Mann," from *Red Suitcase* by Naomi Shihab Nye, copyright © 1994 by Naomi Shihab Nye.

Page 119: HarperCollins Publishers, for permission to reprint an excerpt from "Signals at Sea, " from *Mornings Like This: Found Poems*, by Annie Dillard (page 31). Copyright © 1995 by Annie Dillard. Reprinted by permission of Harper Collins Publishers.

Recommended Reading

FOR COURAGE

Dorothea Brande, *Becoming a Writer*
Natalie Goldberg, *Writing Down the Bones*
Ralph Keyes, *The Courage to Write*
Stephen King, *On Writing*
Anne Lamott, *Bird by Bird*
Carolyn See, *Making a Literary Life*
Twyla Tharp, *The Creative Habit*
Brenda Ueland, *If You Want to Write*

FOR CRAFT

John Gardner, *The Art of Fiction*
Vivian Gornick, *The Situation and the Story*
Mary Oliver, *A Poetry Handbook*
Jane Smiley, *Thirteen Ways of Looking at a Novel*
Jerome Stern, *Making Shapely Fiction*
William Strunk and E. B. White, *The Elements of Style*
William Zinsser, *On Writing Well*

FOR INSPIRATION
Collected Essays

Joan Didion, *The White Album* and *Slouching Towards Bethlehem*
Natalia Ginzburg, *The Little Virtues*
Phillip Lopate, *The Art of the Personal Essay*

Memoir/Autobiography

Joan Didion, *The Year of Magical Thinking*
Mark Doty, *Heaven's Coast* and *Firebird*
Kathryn Harrison, *The Kiss*
Katharine Butler Hathaway, *The Little Locksmith*
James McBride, *The Color of Water*
Carolyn See, *Dreaming*

Poetry

Raymond Carver, *A New Path to the Waterfall*
Billy Collins, *Sailing Alone around the Room*
Donald Hall, *Without*
Jane Kenyon, *Otherwise*
Mary Oliver, *New and Selected Poems*

Autobiographical Fiction

Norman Maclean, *A River Runs through It and Other Stories*

Bibliography

Abbe, Elfrieda, ed. *The Writer's Handbook*. Waukesha, WI: Kalmbach Publishing, updated annually.

Abercrombie, Barbara. *The Show-and-Tell Lion*. New York: Margaret McElderry/Simon and Schuster, 2006.

————. *Writing Out the Storm: Writing Your Way through Serious Illness or Injury*. New York: St. Martin's Press, 2002.

Almquist, Norma. *Plain Sight*. Philadelphia: Xlibris, 2003.

————. *Traveling Light*. Santa Barbara: Fithian Press, 1997.

Alvarez, Julia. *Something to Declare*. New York: Algonquin, 2005.

Atwan, Robert, ed. *The Best American Essays*. Boston: Houghton Mifflin, 1986–2000.

Baker, Russell. "Life with Mother." In *Inventing the Truth*, edited by William Zinsser. Boston: Houghton Mifflin, 1987.

Barron, James. "A Coyote Leads a Crowd on a Central Park Marathon." *New York Times*, March 23, 2006.

Bernard, Andre. *Rotten Rejections: The Letters That Publishers Wish They'd Never Sent*. New York: Pushcart Press, 1990.

Blunt, Judy. *Breaking Clean*. New York: Alfred A.Knopf, 2002.

Bly, Carol. *The Passionate, Accurate Story: Making Your Heart's Truth into Literature*. Minneapolis: Milkweed Editions, 1998.

Brande, Dorothea. *Becoming a Writer*. Los Angeles: J. P. Tarcher, 1981.

Brodie, Deborah, ed. *Writing Changes Everything: The 627 Best Things Anyone Ever Said about Writing*. New York: St. Martin's Press, 1997.

Carver, Raymond. *A New Path to the Waterfall*. New York: Atlantic Monthly Press, 1989.

Collins, Billy. *Sailing Alone around the Room*. New York: Random House, 2001.

Cunningham, Michael. *The Hours*. New York: Farrar, Straus and Giroux, 1998.

Darnton, John, ed. *Writers on Writing: Collected Essays from The New York Times*. New York: Henry Holt, 2001.

Datcher, Michael. *Raising Fences: A Black Man's Love Story*. New York: Riverhead Books, 2001.

Davenport, Nancy. *Eternal Improv*. Lincoln, NB: iUniverse, 2006.

Didion, Joan. *The White Album*. New York: Simon and Schuster, 1979.

————. *The Year of Magical Thinking*. New York: Alfred A. Knopf, 2005.

Dillard, Annie. *Mornings Like This: Found Poems*. New York: HarperCollins, 1995.

————. *The Writing Life*. New York: Harper and Row, 1989.

Doty, Mark. *Dog Years*. New York: HarperCollins, 2007.

————. *Firebird*. New York: Perennial, 1999.

————. *Heaven's Coast*. New York: HarperCollins, 1996.

Dubus, Andre. *Broken Vessels*. Boston: David R. Godine, 1991.

Dunn, Samantha. *Faith in Carlos Gomez: A Memoir of Salsa, Sex, and Salvation*. New York: Henry Holt, 2005.

—————. *Not by Accident: Reconstructing a Careless Life*. New York: Henry Holt, 2002.

Edelman, Hope. *Mother of My Mother: The Intricate Bond between Generations*. New York: Dial Press, 1999.

Epel, Naomi. *Writers Dreaming: 26 Writers Talk about Their Dreams and the Creative Process*. New York: Carol Southern Books, 1993.

Fadiman, Anne. *Ex Libris: Confessions of a Common Reader*. New York: Farrar, Straus and Giroux, 1998.

Gallman, Kuki. *I Dreamed of Africa*. New York: Viking, 1991.

Gardner, John. *The Art of Fiction: Notes on Craft for Young Writers*. New York: Alfred A. Knopf, 1983.

Ginzburg, Natalia. *The Little Virtues*. New York: Little, Brown, 1989.

Glass, Linzi. "Nelson Mandela." Letter to the Editor, *Los Angeles Times*, May 9, 1994.

—————. *The Year the Gypsies Came*. New York: Henry Holt, 2006.

Godwin, Gail. "A Diarist on Diarists." In *Our Private Lives: Journals, Notebooks, and Diaries*, edited by Daniel Halpern. New York: Vintage, 1990.

Goldberg, Natalie. *Writing Down the Bones: Freeing the Writer Within*. Boston: Shambala, 1986.

Gornick, Vivian. *The Situation and the Story: The Art of Personal Narrative*. New York: Farrar, Straus and Giroux, 2002.

Hailey, Elizabeth Forsythe. *Joanna's Husband and David's Wife*. New York: Dell, 1987.

Hall, Donald. *The Best Day the Worst Day: Life with Jane Kenyon*. Boston: Houghton Mifflin, 2005.

———. *Life Work*. Boston: Beacon Press, 1993.

———. *Without*. Boston: Beacon Press, 2002.

Halpern, Daniel, ed. *Our Private Lives: Journals, Notebooks, and Diaries*. New York: Vintage, 1990.

Harden, Blaine. "Suffering and Creativity: Judy Blunt Took Bleakness and Ran with It." *New York Times*, May 28, 2002.

Harrison, Barbara Grizzuti. *The Astonishing World*. New York: Ticknor and Fields, 1992.

Harrison, Kathryn. *The Kiss*. New York: Random House, 1997.

———. *Thicker Than Water*. New York: Random House, 1991.

Haruf, Kent. *Plainsong*. New York: Vintage, 2000.

———. "To See Your Story Clearly, Start by Pulling the Wool over Your Own Eyes." In *Writers on Writing: Collected Essays from The New York Times*, edited by John Darnton. New York: Times Books (Henry Holt), 2001.

Hathaway, Katharine Butler. *The Little Locksmith*. New York: Feminist Press, 2000.

Hazzard, Shirley. *The Transit of Venus*. New York: Penguin, 2000.

Heffron, Jack, ed. *The Best Writing on Writing*. Cincinnati, OH: Story Press, 1994.

Holloway, Monica. *Driving with Dead People*. New York: Simon and Schuster, 2007.

Jurgensen, Geneviève. *The Disappearance*. New York: W. W. Norton, 1999.

Kenyon, Jane. *Otherwise: New and Selected Poems*. St. Paul, MN: Graywolf Press, 1996.

Keyes, Ralph. *The Courage to Write: How Writers Transcend Fear*. New York: Henry Holt, 1995.

King, Stephen. *On Writing: A Memoir of the Craft*. New York: Scribner, 2000.

Kingston, Maxine Hong. *To Be the Poet*. Cambridge, MA: Harvard University Press, 2002.

Kitchen, Judith, and Mary Paumier Jones. *In Brief: Short Takes on the Personal*. New York: W. W. Norton, 1999.

Krementz, Jill, ed. *The Writer's Desk*. New York: Random House, 1996.

Lamott, Anne. *Bird by Bird: Some Instructions on Writing and Life*. New York: Pantheon Books, 1995.

———. *Plan B: Further Thoughts on Faith*. New York: Riverhead Books, 2005.

———. *Traveling Mercies: Some Thoughts on Faith*. New York: Pantheon Books, 1999.

LeClair, Tom, and Larry McCaffery. *Anything Can Happen: Interviews with Contemporary American Novelists*. Chicago: University of Illinois Press, 1988.

Lopate, Phillip. *The Art of the Personal Essay: An Anthology from the Classical Era to the Present*. New York: Doubleday, 1994.

Lynch, Thomas. *Bodies in Motion and at Rest: On Metaphor and Mortality*. New York: W. W. Norton, 2000.

———. "The Going Rate." *New York Times Magazine*, October 15, 2000.

———. *Still Life in Milford*. New York: W. W. Norton, 1999.

Maclean, Norman. *A River Runs through It and Other Stories*. Chicago: University of Chicago Press, 1976.

May, Rollo. *The Courage to Create*. New York: W. W. Norton, 1975.

McBride, James. *The Color of Water: A Black Man's Tribute to His White Mother*. New York: Riverhead Books, 1996.

Mernit, Billy. *Writing the Romantic Comedy*. New York: HarperCollins, 2000.

Minchella, Nancy. *Mama Will Be Home Soon*. New York: Scholastic Press, 2003.

Minot, Stephen. *Three Genres: The Writing of Poetry, Fiction, and Drama*. Englewood Cliffs, NJ: Prentice-Hall, 1965.

Moffat, Mary Jane, and Charlotte Painter, eds. *Revelations: Diaries of Women*. New York: Random House, 1974.

Moore, Lorrie. "Better and Sicker." In *The Agony and the Ego: The Art and Strategy of Fiction Writing Explored*, edited by Clare Boylan. New York: Penguin, 1993.

Morris, Tim. "My Supermarket." *The American Scholar* 69, Winter 2000.

Murdock, Maureen. *Unreliable Truth: On Memoir and Memory*. New York: Seal Press, 2003.

Nash, Jennie. *Raising a Reader: A Mother's Tale of Desperation and Delight*. New York: St. Martin's Press, 2003.

———. *The Victoria's Secret Catalog Never Stops Coming: And Other Lessons I Learned from Breast Cancer*. New York: Scribner, 2001.

Nichols, Jeanne. *Leaning Over the Edge*. Santa Barbara: Fithian Press, 1993.

———. *Running Away from Home and Other Poems*. Philadelphia: Xlibris, 2003.

Norris, Kathleen. *Dakota: A Spiritual Geography*. Boston: Houghton Mifflin, 2001.

Nye, Naomi Shihab. "Valentine for Ernest Mann." In *The Red Suitcase*. Rochester, NY: BOA Editions, 1994.

Oates, Joyce Carol. "Selections from a Journal: January 1985–January 1988." In *Our Private Lives: Journals, Notebooks, and Diaries*, edited by Daniel Halpern. New York: Vintage, 1990.

Oates, Joyce Carol, and Robert Atwan, eds. *The Best American Essays of the Century*. Boston: Houghton Mifflin, 2000.

Oliver, Mary. *New and Selected Poems*. Boston: Beacon Press, 1992.

———. *A Poetry Handbook*. New York: Harcourt Brace and Company, 1994.

Palumbo, Dennis. *Writing from the Inside Out: Transforming Your Psychological Block to Release the Writer Within*. New York: John Wiley and Sons, 2000.

Pollitt, Katha. "Learning to Drive." *New Yorker*, July 22, 2002.

———. "The Webstalker." *New Yorker*, January 19, 2004.

Proulx, Annie, Larry McMurtry, and Diana Ossana. *Brokeback Mountain, Story to Screenplay*. New York: Scribner, 2005.

Robbins, Tom. Interviewed in *On Being a Writer*, edited by Bill Strickland. Cincinnati, OH: Writer's Digest Books, 1989.

Rosenbaum, Lisa Pearl. *A Day of Small Beginnings*. New York: Little, Brown, 2006.

Rosenthal, Amy Krouse. *Encyclopedia of an Ordinary Life*. New York: Crown, 2005.

Rosenthal, Lois. "May Sarton." In *On Being a Writer*, edited

by Bill Strickland. Cincinnati, OH: Writer's Digest
Books, 1989.

Safransky, Sy, ed. *The Sun* magazine. Chapel Hill, NC.

Sarton, May. *Journal of a Solitude*. New York: W. W. Norton,
1973.

Scott-Maxwell, Florida. *The Measure of My Days*. New York:
Alfred A. Knopf, 1972.

Sebold, Alice. *Lucky*. New York: Little, Brown, 1999.

See, Carolyn. *Dreaming: Hard Luck and Good Times in America*. Los Angeles: University of California Press, 1996.

————. *Making a Literary Life: Advice for Writers and Other
Dreamers*. New York: Random House, 2002.

————. *Making History: A Novel*. New York: Houghton
Mifflin, 1991.

Simpson, Mona. In *The Writer's Desk*, edited by Jill Krementz.
New York: Random House, 1996.

Smiley, Jane. *Thirteen Ways of Looking at a Novel*. New York:
Alfred A. Knopf, 2005.

Snyder, Don J. *The Cliff Walk: A Memoir of a Job Lost and a
Life Found*. New York: Little, Brown, 1997.

Stafford, William. *Writing the Australian Crawl: Views on the
Writer's Vocation*. Ann Arbor: University of Michigan
Press, 1978.

Stern, Jerome. *Making Shapely Fiction*. New York: W. W.
Norton, 1991.

Sternburg, Janet, ed. *The Writer on Her Work: Contemporary
Women Writers Reflect on Their Art and Situation*. New
York: W. W. Norton, 1980.

————. *The Writer on Her Work, Volume 2: New Essays in
New Territory*. New York: W. W. Norton, 1991.

St. John, Linda. *Even Dogs Go Home to Die*. New York: HarperCollins, 2001.

Strunk, William, and E. B. White. *The Elements of Style*. New York: Penguin, 2005.

Tharp, Twyla. *The Creative Habit: Learn It and Use It for Life*. New York: Simon and Schuster, 2003.

Thomas, Abigail. *A Three Dog Life*. New York: Harcourt, 2006.

Tyler, Anne. *Celestial Navigation*. New York: Alfred A. Knopf, 1974.

Ueland, Brenda. *If You Want to Write: A Book about Art, Independence and Spirit*. St. Paul, MN: Graywolf Press, 1987.

Walker, Alice. *In Search of Our Mothers' Gardens: Womanist Prose*. New York: Harvest Books, 1984.

Winspear, Jacqueline. *Messenger of Truth*. New York: Henry Holt, 2006.

Zackheim, Victoria, ed. *For Keeps: Women Tell the Truth about Their Bodies, Growing Older, and Acceptance*. San Francisco: Seal Press, 2007.

Zinsser, William. *On Writing Well*. New York: Harper and Row, 1976.

———. *Writing about Your Life: A Journey into the Past*. New York: Marlowe and Company, 2004.

About the Author

Barbara Abercrombie's most recent books are *Writing Out the Storm*, a memoir and writing guide published by St. Martin's Press, and *The Show-and-Tell Lion*, a picture book published by Margaret McElderry/Simon and Schuster. She has also published two novels for adults and seven books for children, including the award-winning picture book *Charlie Anderson*. Her novels have been optioned for films and published in six languages, and her essays, articles, and poems have appeared in numerous magazines and newspapers, including the *Los Angeles Times*, the *Christian Science Monitor*, and the *Baltimore Sun*.

She teaches in the Writers' Program at UCLA Extension and conducts writing workshops for the Wellness Community, a nationwide cancer support group. With her daughter Brooke Abercrombie, she has created a writing website with ongoing advice and inspiration for writers: www.WritingTime.net.